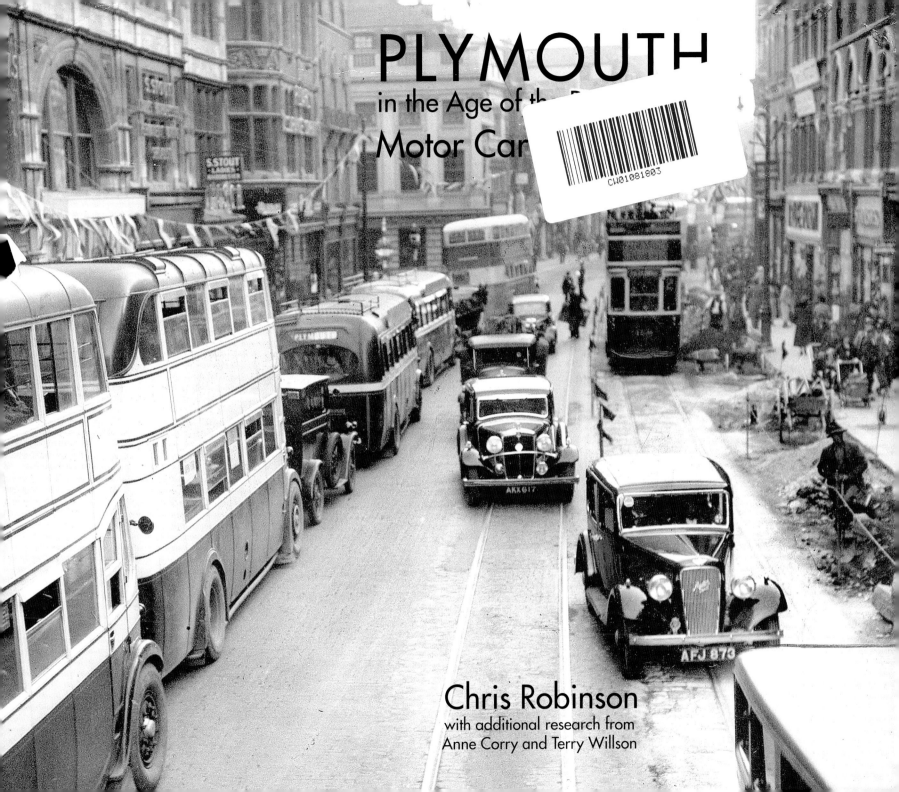

PLYMOUTH
in the Age of the
Motor Car

Chris Robinson
with additional research from
Anne Corry and Terry Willson

British Library in Publication Data
Robinson, Chris 1954 –
PLYMOUTH IN THE AGE OF THE PETROL-DRIVEN MOTOR CAR
1896-1939

A catalogue record for this book is available from the British Library
ISBN 978-1-9160190-6-5

Content, Layout & Design
Chris Robinson
Cover design by Benji Robinson
© Chris Robinson 2021

First published November 2021

Front cover image:
Plymouth Embankment Toll Gate 1 April 1924
Back cover main images:
Spooner's Corner c1937
Francis Pearse's Benz 1931

Published by
Pen & Ink Publishing
34 New Street, Barbican
Plymouth PL1 2NA
Tel: 01752 705337
www.chrisrobinson.co.uk

Printed and bound in Great Britain by:
Short Run Press Limited
25 Bittern Road
Sowden Industrial Estate
Exeter, EX2 7LW
01392 211909 www.shortrunpress.co.uk

CONTENTS

'View of Plymouth from the Old London Road showing a portion of the Seven Trees' for centuries the main road into town from the east, wide enough for a coach and horses.

INTRODUCTION

'The automobile changed our dress, manners, social customs, vacation habits, the shape of our cities, consumer purchase patterns, common tastes and positions in intercourse'.
John Keats The Insolent Chariots

It is a few years now since someone first asked me if I might consider writing a book about local garages and car showrooms. At the time I was somewhat dismissive of the idea, as indeed was my dear wife and publisher, Clare, however I did think about the prospect and the more I thought about it, the more I warmed to the notion.

With the future of the petrol-driven motor car constantly under the spotlight these days and with the expectation that we should all go electric within the next decade or so, it occurred to me that in the grand scheme of things the petrol-driven motor car might come to have a history that was even shorter than the age of coach and horses. What's more, none of the twentieth century Plymouth history books have even bothered to mention the impact that the petrol-driven motor car has had on our day-to-day lives. Newspapers, cinemas, radio stations and television providers may merit a little bit of attention, but there is little or no reference to the impact of electricity or the telephone or supermarkets and even less to the motor car.

Is it because these aspects of our existence are too universal to relate to the particular, too big to examine in the context of our city?

Somewhere Crispin Gill spoke of the Admiralty vetoing the plans of a leading car manufacturer that wanted to come here in the 1920s, on the grounds that it would create unwelcome competition for the Dockyard, but that was about it. However certain local car dealers would come to make a fortune from the industry – especially the likes of William Mumford, Frank Barton and AC Turner.

Furthermore the motor car has completely transformed the way we live: it required us to built better roads, with better surfaces and wider highways. Where once there may have been a narrow, little used track that only one vehicle could pass through in any one direction at a time, soon we had carriageways wide enough to allow movement freely in both directions at the same time, and then dual carriageways and then three or four lane motorways. Somehow the motor car insinuated itself on society from the 1890s onwards, just as, a century later, the internet did.

The question is, would we have had the internet without the model created by the combustion engine?

Photograph dated around 1924 of the first vehicle in Plymouth to be officially registered in 1904, the car is a then brand new Argyll made in Glasgow.

Suddenly we could move around the countryside faster than ever before. We could shift goods and services independently of the railway network. Trains had opened up places that had hitherto been all but inaccessible, but the combustion engine opened up even more.

But that opening up wasn't just limited to a bigger and better interconnecting network of roads, as the combustion engine proved capable of lifting vehicles off the ground and into the air. Truth be told a steam-driven aeroplane was never on the cards and while the first great steam train, Stevenson's *Rocket*, may have given its name to a special kind of craft capable of going beyond the earth's atmosphere, coal was never going to be a practical source of rocket fuel and you don't need to be a rocket scientist to work that out!

And so the combustion engine gave us Benz's original three-wheeled motorwagen, powered flight and the ability to put a man on the moon. This opening up of lines of communications across countries, continents and the planets, created an interconnected network that is echoed in our understanding of how the brain functions and underpins the workings of the internet.

It has given us artificial intelligence that can solve problems quicker than we can ... but don't ask it to solve the problem of climate change as AI is part of the problem, not the solution. A robot will never recommend its own destruction and anyway the solution lies with Mother Nature not with Science and Technology, as it's far too late for that.

Would we have been able to create something like the internet without the example of our interconnecting network of vehicular pathways along which we all travel – our fibre optic motorways? Who knows, but I doubt it. The motor car changed the very way we interact with the world and think about it.

It may seem like it was luxury only available to the wealthy and well to do at first, but it very soon became a democratising tool. Within a generation of the practical application of the combustion engine there were hundreds of cars on the road. A generation later there were tens of thousands of cars and then millions.

'Glorious, stirring sight!' murmured Toad, nevering offering to move. 'The poetry of motion! The real way to travel! The only way to travel! Here to-day – in next week to-morrow! Villages skipped, towns and cities jumped – always somebody else's horizon! O bliss! O poop-poop! O my! O my!'
'O stop being an ass, Toad!' cried the Mole despairingly.

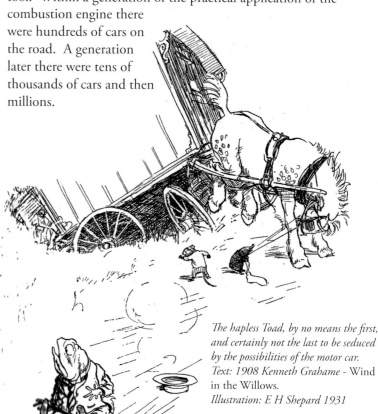

The hapless Toad, by no means the first, and certainly not the last to be seduced by the possibilities of the motor car.
Text: 1908 Kenneth Grahame - Wind in the Willows.
Illustration: E H Shepard 1931

Today there are over 40 million vehicles licensed in the UK, servicing slightly less than 70 million residents.

Since 2000 there have been more households with two or more cars or vans than those with none. The average age of all of those vehicles is between 8.0-9.3 years – so there is a lot of obsolescence However, motor vehicles allow us to carry more shopping than we would carry on foot, to work wherever we like, spend leisure time when and where we want, holiday wherever and not worry too much about the weather in our choice of clothing as we travel in warm and dry, or cool and comfortable car interiors.

The motor car also means that clandestine meetings are easier to arrange. You can't readily imagine drug traffickers taking the train – the county lines don't refer to train lines.

And then there are the illicit romances. Time was when every town or city had a 'love lane' somewhere on the edge of town where courting couples could meet discreetly on foot – Plymouth had more than one – but the motor car, and the motorcycle, conferred a new found freedom and possibly did more for democracy than universal suffrage.

So how can this story be told through Plymouth and its surroundings? The same way that any story concerning this scepter'd isle can be told, by examining what happened right under our very noses. Plymouth is no different to any other British city. We may not have had a major motor manufacturer on our doorstep – notwithstanding Mumfords – but our experience of the motor car, how we welcomed it, how we coped with it, how we drew up measures to deal with it, are issues that are as relevant here as they were anywhere. So sit back and enjoy finding out how that story unfolded over the first 40 years or so. Where possible I have endeavoured to use contemporary accounts as they convey the thinking back then far better than we can do today with that distorted lens we call hindsight.

Read all about Plymouth's pioneering car manufacturer who was as successful in the early days of car production as Henry Ford, read of Plymouth's link to the man who brought the first car into

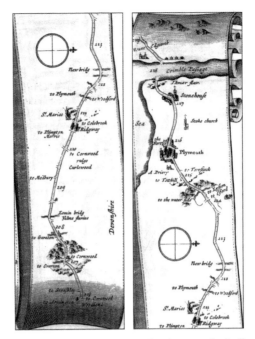

The Cornwood to Stonehouse Road as drawn up by Ogilby

In 1675 John Ogilby produced Britain's first road atlas. Prior to Ogilby's efforts, maps of English counties made little or no reference to highways or byways, only to various principal seats of the landed gentry, towns, villages and, significantly, rivers.

There was also, pre-Ogilby, no general agreement on measurement. There were Roman miles – literally milia passum –1,000 paces (1,680 yards) long miles (2,428 yards), local miles (variable) and the shorter occasional mile of 1,760 yards. The latter was the one adopted by Ogilby and this then became the standard measurement.

The strip opposite, divided here in two, is one of 100 strips that Ogilby's team produced for his 1675 Britannia Atlas. His brief had been to 'depict the Post Roads for conveying letters to and from London.' Ogilby's maps were subsequently used as the basis for a number of guides to English roads for the next 100 years.

the country, read too about the eccentric dentist who brought the first car into Plymouth.

Find out where and why Plymouth's first traffic lights were erected, the first one-way street created and the first car park laid out. And all the while think about how much our four-wheeled friends have shifted the world away from our natural environment and set us along an unrelenting road to an unsustainable future.

Chris Robinson MBE
Plymouth
November 2021

THE PETROL-DRIVEN MOTOR CAR IS JUST AROUND THE CORNER

It's hard now to imagine a world without cars, however 100 years ago there were hardly any on the streets of Plymouth, or any other city for that matter. What's more although the petrol-driven motor car had been around since the German engineer Karl Benz patented his first machine in Mannheim back in 1886 their spread was comparatively slow at first. It wasn't until 1894 that the first car appeared on a British public highway and that was a two-horse-power Benz 'Patent Motor Velocipede'. Purchased for around £80 (approx. £10,000 today) it was the prize possession of a London tea/coffee merchant called Henry Hewetson who drove his vehicle quite freely in and around Catford for a few weeks without any problem ... until he was warned by the local Police Inspector that he would be charged unless he acted in accordance with the 1865 'Locomotives on Highways Act' which required that the car should be preceded along the highway by a pedestrian waving a red flag.

So it was that the enterprising Mr Heweston engaged the services of two lads, one of whom sat with him in his car, while the other cycled ahead looking out for bobbies on the beat – and, as soon as the old bill had been clocked he would give the other lad a signal and he would then jump down from the car, walk briskly ahead of his master flamboyantly waving a two-inch-square of red linen fixed to a pencil, until the policeman was out of sight.

Remarkably, Heweston was one of only two motorists in England in 1894, the following year a few more followed, mainly driving imported vehicles, although that year also saw the production of Britain's first home-built petrol-driven motor cars. JH Knight, Herbert Austin, Frederick Lanchester and JD Roots were the respective pioneer manufacturers and by the end of 1895 estimates suggest that there around 14-15 such vehicles on our roads ... factor in a handful of steam-driven and electric vehicles cars and you perhaps had 20 altogether.

That number was to rise dramatically over the next few years however, and by the turn of the century it was estimated that there were maybe as many as 800 cars in Britain, most of them in and around London and the Home Counties. The Continent, by comparison, was way ahead of the game with some 5,000 vehicles in France alone.

Beyond the pocket of all but a few, those people who could afford a car were also prime candidates to splash out on literature about the new phenomenon, particularly as ownership statistics continued their spectacular rise. Indeed, such was the speed of change that in the July 1902 edition of *Autocar* (first published in November 1895) it was reported that 'Last week a member of our staff, whilst in the West End, counted 23 cars within three-quarters of an hour.'

Not surprisingly there were accidents, and as the number of cars increased so did the number of casualties, particularly among pedestrians. Small wonder therefore that in 1903 the Motor Car Act came into being, requiring every motorcar to be registered with a corresponding, visible, number plate. The notion had been introduced in Holland five years earlier and with the highest number of vehicles in England at that time being in London, that was where the plate A1 was issued – it was snapped up by Frank Russell, the 2nd Earl Russell, a celebrated early enthusiast of the motoring age.

In Plymouth Francis Henry Pearse, a dental surgeon of this parish, was hailed as the first to drive a car on our local streets. It seems that he bought his Benz in 1901, but when registration plates were first issued it wasn't a question of the oldest vehicle having the earliest number and the registration plate on his car was CO 53. CO was the original Plymouth plate prefix so it would be interesting to know who those people were who had the numbers CO 1 to CO 52.

Mutley Plain early 1900s – it was on 4 April 1901 that the tram route along the Plain, which had been horse drawn since 1895, was electrified.

Few cities have witnessed as many changes to their central street layout over the years as Plymouth has but here, at the southern end of Mutley Plain we have a stretch that has been remarkably consistent throughout the twentieth century and beyond and this sequence of images wonderfully captures the impact that the petrol-driven motor car had between the arrival of the electric tram at the dawn of the 1900s through to the 1930s.

From a busy but human and horse-powered thoroughfare this main northern route out of Plymouth gradually gave way to the latest incarnation of wheeled transport.

Although undated, the picture at the bottom of this page was in all likelihood taken in or before 1913 (as that is the postal date on the reverse side of the original) and doubtless a decade or so after the image above it.

The car moving away from the photographer, bearing the number plate CO 62 was issued in 1907 but since reallocated as the vehicle bearing the number is a Rover 12 dating from 1913.

By the time the photograph on the opposite page was taken more than 5000 vehicles had been given a CO plate. The car on the left here appears to have the number CO 5885, making it a 1923 registration and such was the rate at which cars were being bought that by 1926 the range of four digit CO numbers had been exhausted and the DR prefix (originally intended for Devonport registrations and temporarily halted when the Three Towns amalgamated and the Great War began) was reintroduced for local registrations. The van in the middle of the image here bears a DR plate and is clearly not a pre-1914 vehicle.

We are still in the early days of motoring however, although there is no shortage of signage around – most notably the consistent end wall Plymouth Co-operative advertisement. There are no obvious road signs or any form of indication suggesting where those on foot might cross this busy road, hence the presence of pedestrians in the road in all three of these images.

Top: Mutley Plain c1901 Bottom: Same view c1913 – note the sign on the lamppost All Cars Stop a sign for tramcars rather than motorcars – the car in the foreground is a new two-seater Rover 12, the CO 2 plate has been re-used.. Opposite page: Mutley late-1920s

Top: Horse tram 'To & From Market Place, Mutley & Compton Lane, 1896
Bottom: Heading up North Hill with a 'cock horse' (as in 'Ride a Cock Horse to
Banbury Cross') an extra beast engaged to help pull the tram up the incline.

HORSE TRAMS

In the centenary edition of the *Western Independent* in an article entitled 'Plymouth Then and Now' Henry Vigurs Harris who had been born into a local decorating and picture-dealing family back in 1851, discussed the many changes he had witnessed.

The chief difference between the town of 1833 and 1933 he averred, was 'its means of communication. No railways, no trams, no motors, no electricity. Horse did everything.

'True,' he added, 'there were not wanting enthusiastic people who at least foresaw steam traction.

'In 1829 Sir Goldsworthy Gurney, the Cornish inventor, having applied his steamblast principal to Trevithick's steam road carriage, made a journey in it from London to Bath and back at 15 miles an hour; and in 1831 Sir Charles Dance ran a public steam carriage of Gurney's manufacture five times a day between Gloucester and Cheltenham for several months, carrying thousands of passengers, without mishap.

'More locally still,' he said, 'Mr Thomas Lee Stevens, of Plymouth, proposed that a similar carriage should be run between Plymouth and Devonport, and doubtless it would have been done if a reactionary Parliament had not stepped in and stopped the whole development in the interest of the stage coaches.

'For this reason, the horse remained supreme in the street traffic of Plymouth for another half century.'

Notwithstanding that fact Plymouth was one of the first towns in Britain to operate a horse tramway. Indeed the Plymouth, Stonehouse & Devonport Tramways Company – the first to have been formed after the Parliamentary Tramway Acto of 1870 – has been described as the 'grandfather of all legitimate tramway companies.'

It commenced operations on 18 March 1872. From the horse's perspective tramlines made pulling carriages much easier and smoother whatever the weather. However it meant they could also haul heavier loads, great from the punter's perspective, because the cost of using public transport came down, but not necessarily for the horse.

Posing for the photographer at West Hoe c1895.

Top: Alderman W T Jinkin with his preferred mode of transport outside his home, No7 Lipson Terrace, August 1924. Bottom: Youngsters with their horse and cart in Citadel Road.

UNSTABLE SITUATION?

For many years after the introduction of the motor car the horse and cart or carriage remained a conspicuous sight on city streets. In some instances this was not just because people couldn't afford to purchase petrol-guzzling machines, it was because they didn't want to. One of Plymouth's most ardent embracers of all things equine was the distinguished property developer, builder and philanthropist William Thomas Jinkin.

In 1911, Jinkin, although one of the few people locally who could easily afford a motor car, invited the architectural practice of Carder & Carder to draw up proposals for an extension to his coach-house at Lipson Terrace.

An inveterate horse-lover, who insisted on going everywhere in his carriage and pair, he was determined to resist the drive to modern transport, and even toured England and Scotland behind his dung droppers. Hunting on horseback into his 80s, he could still be seen riding around the streets of Plymouth on his mount in 1935, aged 87.

Meanwhile among the many businesses, that persisted with horse-power well into the twentieth century were the Plymouth Co-operative Society, who had large stables at Peverell, Great Western Railways and Pooley's Bakery, who built a substantial stable block at Woodside, not far from their new bakehouse in Egerton Road. However the era of the horse as a key part of commercial transportation was coming to end despite any Canute like efforts being exercised on their behalf and nowhere was this more graphically illustrated than in 1928, when Richard Barton's marketing team deployed 'a novel method of introducing the new Morris Minor 8 horse-power' – they harnessed four pairs of horses to a cart carrying the new motor for a publicity shot.

For the general public, what better way was there to demonstrate that the motor car had four times greater pulling power than that of the two hardy creatures previously needed to haul heavy trams around the Three Towns?

Top: A handful of Pooley's horse-drawn bread vans outside their Woodside stables. Bottom: The Barton Motor Co Ltd, utilize an unusual method of introducing the new Morris Minor 8 horse-power saloon.

EVELYN HENRY ELLIS

While Plymothians may not have seen the first petrol-driven motor car ever introduced into this country, they certainly did see the man responsible. The Honourable Eveyln Henry Ellis was born at the British Embassy in Portugal on 9 August 1843. He was the fifth son of Charles Augustus Ellis (6th Baron Howard de Walden and 2nd Baron Seaford) and his wife Lucy Joan Cavendish.

In 1857 the young Evelyn joined the Royal Navy as a cadet and doubtless came to know the port reasonably well – he was certainly stationed here, in the Hamoaze, in 1861. Three years later, and now a midshipman, he left the service. It would appear that he returned to the continent for a number of years and in 1882 he married Alberta Mary Hardinge (the daughter of the 4th Duke of Portland) in Nice, France.

In June 1895, now in his early fifties, Evelyn ordered a left-hand drive motor car, to be made to his own specifications, from the Paris firm of Panhard-Levassor.

The car, like so many at that time had a 3.5 hp Daimler engine, it also had solid rubber tyres.

The following month he had the vehicle shipped to the British mainland and together with his driving companion, Frederick Simms, the two made the first horseless, petrol-driven carriage drive on English roads. Simms gave a glorious account of the journey in an article for the *Saturday Review* on 11 July 1895: 'We set forth at exactly 9.26 am and made good progress on the well-made old London coaching road; it was delightful travelling on that fine summer morning. We were not without anxiety as to how the horses we might meet would behave towards their new rivals, but they took it very well and out of 133 horses we passed only two little ponies did not seem to appreciate the innovation. On our way we passed a great many vehicles of all kinds (ie horse-drawn), as well as cyclists.

'It was a very pleasing sensation to go along the delightful roads towards Virginia Water at speeds varying from 3-23 miles per hour, and our iron horse behaved splendidly. There we took our luncheon and fed our engine with a little oil. Going down the steep hill leading to Windsor we passed through Datchet and arrived right in front of the entrance hall of Mr Ellis's house at Datchet at 5.40, thus completing our most enjoyable journey of 56 miles, the first ever made by a petroleum motor carriage in this country, in 5 hours 32 minutes, exclusive of stoppages and at an average speed of 9.84 mph.

'In every place we passed through we were not unnaturally the objects of a great deal of curiosity. Whole villages turned out to behold, open-mouthed, the new marvel of locomotion. The departure of coaches was delayed to enable their passengers to have a look at our horseless vehicle, while cyclists would stop to gaze enviously at us as we surmounted with ease some long hill. 'Mr Ellis's motor carriage is a neat and compact four-wheeled dog-cart with accommodation for four persons and two portmanteau. The consumption of petroleum is little over a halfpenny per mile and there is no smoke, heat or smell, the carriage running smoothly and without any vibration.'

1910 this car appeared in a letter from D C Defries stating that the car is owned by Vaughan Williams and asking for help to raise funds of £100 to purchase it and then to donate it to the Science Museum.

Having described himself as a 'loafer' in the 1911 census, when he was staying in the Gloster Hotel in Weymouth, it appears that he soon afterwards decamped to the town he has spent some time in during his younger years, for in September 1913, when he died, in the Grand Hotel on the Hoe, he was described as having been living in Plymouth for 14 months. A report in the *Western Evening Herald* noted 'that he had travelled about the world a great deal, keeping for the most part away from the beaten track of tourists, and had some very interesting experiences.' Not least of which was having the 'honour of giving the late King Edward VII his first ride in an automobile.'

The arrival of this new machine in England created a fair amount of excitement in Ellis's home neighbourhood. A couple of weeks after its debut the *Windsor & Eton Express* featured an article entitled Datchet: A Horseless Carriage. The author went into a degree of technical detail before painting a broader picture:

'If anyone cares to run over to Datchet they will see the Hon. Evelyn Ellis of 'Rosenau' careering around the roads, up hill and down dale, and without danger to life and limb, in his new motor carriage which he brought over a short time ago from Paris where they are in pretty frequent use.

'Can it be easily driven? We cannot say that such a vehicle would be suitable for a lady, unless rubber-tyred wheels and other improvements are made to the carriage, for a firm grip of the steering-handle and a keen eye are necessary for its safe guidance. But for gentlemen they would be invaluable, especially if they were used, as they are on the Continent, by doctors and commercial travellers. Is there fear of accident? It need not be apprehended that this new vehicle, if it becomes popular, will cause any dangerous alarm to horses. Already accustomed to the incidents and surprises of everyday street traffic they would soon become as indifferent to horseless carriages, silent and unobtrusive, as they already are to bicycles.

'What is its cost? Such a one as that owned by the Hon Evelyn Ellis would cost £200, and for long journeys its maintenance would be from ten pence to a shilling an hour.

'It is a splendid hill climber and climbs at a faster pace than a pedestrian can walk. A trip from Rosenau to Old Windsor, up Priest Hill and descending the steep, rough and dangerous hill on the opposite side, past the workhouse and through Old Windsor back to Rosenau within an hour demonstrates how perfectly under control this carriage is, while the sensation of being whirled rapidly along is decidedly pleasing.'

Ellis was keen to see the motor industry develop in England and spent around £20,000 (around £2.5m today) supporting some of the earliest established companies and when the Automobile Club was established here in 1897 he was one of the first members and was elected as one of two vice-chairmen.

One wonders who he met in his last 14 months spent in Plymouth but clearly he had many tales to tell, including the time, during one of his early driving exploits around Windsor:

'One old stonebreaker threw down his hammer and threw up his arms in amazement as he saw the carriage approaching him and said, "Well, I'm blessed if Mother Shipton's prophecy ain't come true. Here comes carriage without horse".'

Ellis in an 1895 Panhard.

THOMAS BUCKLAND JEFFERY - PLYMOUTH'S GREATEST CAR MAKER

1891 ad for the American Rambler cycles.
.Rambler.

1896 ad for the Bicycle Riding Academie.

Thomas Jeffery and his family in a 1902

Thomas Buckland Jeffery was born on 5 February 1845, at 3 Mill Pleasant Road, Stoke Damerel (on the site near the Edgcumbe Arms), to Thomas Hellier and Elizabeth Buckland Jeffery. Thomas was their second child and first of four sons.

His name hasn't been greatly celebrated locally but it turns out that Jeffery became a giant of the early American motor industry and left an estate valued at $3 million in 1910.

A bright young man with a 'hunger to make things,' Thomas served an apprenticeship in an instrument maker's shop in Plymouth, before deciding, at 18, to chance his arm in America. He found work with a firm of instrument makers in Chicago, creating models of various pieces of scientific equipment – microscopes, telescopes or whatever else inventors were filing patents for and needed a model to go with the application. Not only did it afford Thomas some useful practical experience, learning from other people's mistakes, but it also appears to have been quite well paid and he had soon earned enough to open his own premises – which he lost in the great Chicago fire of 1871.

So he briefly went back to microscope manufacture, to build up his funds again.

Not long after opening his second shop he married a local girl, Kate Wray, and soon Thomas turned his attention to the business of making – and repairing – carriages. Later his imagination was fired up by the idea of manufacturing a two-wheeled transporter. A trip back to Blighty (he regularly sent money home) had acquainted him with his first penny farthing and, by the end of the 1870s, Jeffery's first bicycle was on sale, The American. While the creating of these machines fascinated him, the paperwork didn't and he recruited another Plymouth exile, an old school friend from back home, R Philip Gormully. So was born the Gormully-Jeffery partnership and a range of new bicycles.

In 1891 Thomas Jeffery came up with an invention of his own, and one that would make a fortune for the G&J Tire Company (set up to manufacture the product and which ultimately became part of United States Rubber) – the pneumatic tyre. This was one patent that Jeffery fought hard to protect, successfully in the

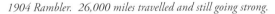

1904 Rambler. 26,000 miles travelled and still going strong.

Three vehicles, one chassis.

Rambling on his mind, early model. Inset below: 1916 Rambler.

States, but not in Britain, despite taking the matter to the House of Lords.

Nevertheless business boomed and Gormully & Jeffery became the second-largest bicycle company in America. Their bicycles became known as Ramblers (named after Jeffery's horse) and were very popular.

In time Gormully died and Jeffery sold out to the only firm bigger than his, Albert Pope. He received 'a princely sum' and invested in one of his old, and already abandoned, bicycle factories in Winsconsin. His aim: to create a new Rambler, a four-wheeled automotive one.

His eldest son, Charles, had now joined him and the motorcar was still very much in its infancy, indeed most models were notoriously unreliable: 'All unnecessary, that can be cured,' was the Jeffery verdict – as he proved.

Within a year or two he was producing cars that could reach an average speed of 30 mph and went on to turn out thousands of cars every year.

All the while he introduced key modifications; a steering wheel, spare wheel, a petrol gauge (which obviated the need for 'a stick or the like to estimate the amount of fuel in the tank') and four-wheel-drive Quad, an instant success.

Charles Jeffery was by this time in control, his father having died. Charles might have taken the company on to much bigger things still had it not been for a life-changing experience on the ill-fated Lusitania in 1915 (he was one of 761 survivors – 1198 lives were lost when the liner was torpedoed by a German submarine), prompting him to retire at the age of 40.

So it was that Charles Jeffery sold the company to Charles Nash, hence the later Nash Rambler (of Beep Beep song fame) and other Rambler cars manufactured by the American Motors Corporation, until they were bought out by Chrysler in 1987. Meanwhile Jeffery's original factory in Kenosha (Wisconsin) was used for car production for 108 years, only closing in 2010.

Albert Road, c1905, close examination shows the wording 'Kimber's Garage' in the first block on the left, while on the gable end of the building further down on the left the word 'cycle' can be clearly deciphered, but note no bicycles, motorcycles or motor cars appear in the scene.

KIMBER'S
DEVONPORT'S FIRST GARAGE?

Uriah Kimber arrived in Devonport sometime in the mid-1870s when he was in his mid-twenties. A blacksmith from Northlew, near the aptly named East Kimber, to the north of Okehampton, Uriah appears to have taken root in Albert Road and for a while worked his trade in the Dockyard.

In 1876 he married Eliza Honey, a young Cornish maid, four years his senior, in Devonport, and before long they had added eight children to their happy household. John Kimber, born on 31 May 1877 was their eldest son, and by the time John was old enough to join his father at work, Uriah had forsaken his original trade for that of a cycle dealer.

Father and son took business premises at 29 Albert Road, down towards the Dockyard's Albert Road Gate and, with cycling rapidly gaining in popularity, the enterprise thrived. Like so many other cycle dealers of their day, it wasn't long before they had embraced the first generation of motorcycles and then the early motor car.

With William Mumford moving into Albert Road there was little doubt that this was a prime outlet for the four-wheelers as well as the two-wheelers and by 1907 the Kimbers were already styling themselves as cycle and motor dealers. By the early 1920s Kimber's Garage was proudly advertising all makes of Ford cars in stock, with the added boast that they were the 'oldest authorized Ford Dealers in the West.'

The very first Fords (three Model As) had been imported into this country in 1903 and the very first British dealership was opened in Southampton in 1910, this being a year before a British assembly plant was established in an old tram factory at Trafford Park, Manchester, to produce Henry Ford's Model Ts.

By this time John and his young family had moved to Queen's

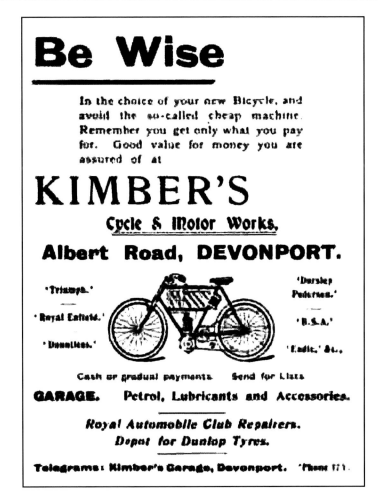

Gate overlooking Victoria Park, while Uriah had moved to Hilary Terrace in Stoke. The motor industry was clearly serving the family well and Kimber & Sons moved into purpose built premises on the corner of Exmouth Road and Albert Road, just up from the Tramway Shelter and the London & South Western Railway halt.

The business carried on under the Kimber banner for several decades.

FRANCES LATIMER
PLYMOUTH'S FIRST LADY CYCLIST

In the early 1890s it was claimed that a certain Selina Frances Latimer (right), a somewhat feisty Plymouth woman in her early 40s was the first English lady to ride a bicycle. An interesting claim to fame and one that was repeated in the *Portsmouth Evening News* of 9 September 1899 when they said that this particular distinction was claimed for Miss Frances Latimer of Plymouth who began riding in 1891.

However on the very same day, in September 1899, in Cumberland, the *Penrith Observer* noted that 'now Miss B A Masters of Torquay had come forward to say that she had been riding twice as long as Miss Latimer'.

Miss Masters was quoted as saying 'I rode sociable tricycles from 1883 to 1885, tandem bicycles from 1885 to 1887. Then I went for single tricycles which I rode until February 1889, ten and a half years ago, when I had one of the best ladies' safeties made for the use of English women, and from then till today I have ridden bicycles all the year round.'

It would be interesting, noted the journalist responsible for the piece, to know 'whether there are ladies who can show a longer record than that of Miss Masters.'

Apparently there was, although there is no indication that the lady concerned ever wrote in to the *Penrith Observer* to make

the claim. Jeanie Welford (nee Morgan) was evidently just 25 in 1880 when she became the first female member of the British Bicycle Touring Club (later to become Cycling UK). Jeanie, from the West Midlands, appears to have been introduced to the Club by her brother Stanley (right), who used to take her on social tricycle outings. Her interest in such wheeled transport was doubtless consolidated soon after joining the club as she married a fellow club member Richard Welford from Newcastle upon Tyne.

The cycling craze was essentially a French phenomenon that began in the early 1860s, although the credit for creating the first pedal cycle goes to a Scotsman, Kirkpatrick Macmillan who produced his first machine back in 1839 and regularly rode his machine around Dumfries. Indeed when completing a 40-mile cycle to Glasgow in the summer of 1842 he accidentally knocked over a child who was part of a crowd that had turned out to see his 'iron horse'. He was fined five shillings for the offence!

Curiously enough it was around this time that his niece also started riding his machine and so, technically, Mary Marchbank was Britain's first lady cyclist.

However all these early contenders for the title shouldn't suggest that women cyclists were a common sight on the streets, or even an acceptable face of femininity.

In November 1894, an article in a series in *The Comet* on 100 local notable figures, observed of Miss Latimer (only the second woman ever to be featured after Aggie Weston) that although she was to be seen regularly bicycling around the town, the activity had 'not yet "caught on" in the Three Towns,' although it was becoming 'more and more general in the United Kingdom'. Miss Latimer, ran the article, 'looks forward in running the gauntlet of street witticism and animadversion to smooth the way for local women's enjoyment of this helpful and exhilarating exercise' and is hopeful that 'in the coming spring others will follow her example and that Plymouth will possess a women's cycling club'.

At that time Plymouth did not exactly possess a plethora of cycle outlets – there was Henry Blight and George Duggua, both in Raleigh Street (how apt!) and Charles Frank in Station Road, Stoke. There was also one local cycle manufacturer, Albert Martin in King Street. By the end of the nineteenth century there would be a whole lot of dealers across the Three Towns, including Brooks, in Ebrington Street; Griffiths in Frankfort Street; CJ Hall on Eldad Hill; Robert Humm, and Lott & Robb both in Old Town Street; Kimbers in Albert Road, Morice Town; Parkhouse in Battery Street, Stonehouse; Pomeroy & Co and Reed & Co in the Stonehouse end of Union Street, and Yabsley in King Street. Miss Latimer meanwhile was becoming increasingly focussed on pedalling the notion of Votes for Women. The only daughter of the celebrated newspaper proprietor, printer, councillor and Plymouth Mayor, Isaac Latimer, Miss Latimer was a prominent figure on the national Suffrage scene and an eminent author in her own right, she was also the first, or at least one of the first, women to become an Associate of the Institute of Journalists and she used to take her guitar along to Liberal Association meetings. Doubtless if anyone did come out with any witticism as she cycled past, she would have had an appropriate riposte.

Unidentified Plymouth lady cyclist, c1903 although the bicycle is a c1896 model fitted with Bowden rear brake (c1898).

FULL STEAM AHEAD?

Steam-driven vehicles were by no means unknown on the streets of Plymouth – the Co-op purchased their first such machine in 1908. Despite initial disappointments concerning the loading that the vehicle was able to safely and successfully transport they continued to deploy steam lorries for the next couple of decades at least. Many other firms for whom haulage was an issue did so too, among them Huxham & Co. Although they concurrently employed petrol-driven machines they also persisted, well into the 1920s, with horses as well.

However one wonders what impact one particular incident in August 1928 had on the management's attitude to the steam machines: 'As a steam lorry belonging to Huxham and Co, was proceeding over Stonehouse Bridge from Devonport the steering gear apparently refused to function, with the result that the lorry ran into the side of the bridge, dislodging a large masonry pillar and smashing part of the concrete path.

'Evidently the impact with the pillar prevented the front of the lorry from crashing into the wall of the Bridge Inn. As it was the front of the vehicle overhung the bridge, four or five feet below which is a footpath that separates the public house from the bridge railings. The lorry was pulled back to the road by a Corporation tramcar and later it was towed away. Neither driver nor steersman was hurt.'

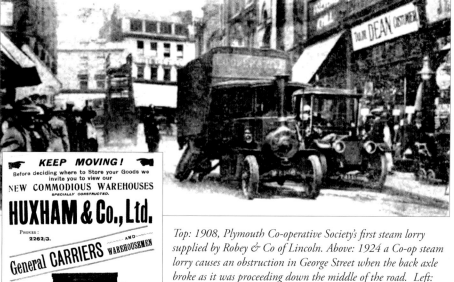

Top: 1908, Plymouth Co-operative Society's first steam lorry supplied by Robey & Co of Lincoln. Above: 1924 a Co-op steam lorry causes an obstruction in George Street when the back axle broke as it was proceeding down the middle of the road. Left: 1925 ad for Huxham & Co. Right: August 1928 a Huxham steam lorry is involved in a most unfortunate accident.

Devonport Corporation was another early adopter of the steam lorry, purchasing a number of Mann's Patent Steam Cart & Wagon Co Ltd vehicles from their Leeds-based factory. Steam wagons were invariably slow to start as the water had to be boiled in order to generate a head of steam. This was not a quick process. They were also 'dirty' as they used coal as a heat source and belched smoke. They were also heavy with, initially, solid wheels. Steam lorries, however, although uncommon were not rare and survived on the streets long after the first generation of steam cars had been forsaken in favour of the petrol-driven version particularly after the introduction of the electric starter, which eliminated the risk of the potentially wrist-damaging need to hand crank the engine.

Steam rollers, on the other hand, which were made to be slow and heavy enjoyed a working life that outlasted all other incarnations of steam-powered road vehicles.

Above: Two vehicles owned by the pre-Amalgamation Devonport Corporation Cleansing Department. U 2510 and U 2511. Top right: U 3373 Another Mann's machine, hence the Leeds licence plate, this one bought by Chaplins of Devonport (Mann's were sold to Scammel in 1930). Right: A classic Aveling Barford Invicta steamroller, with the celebrated prancing horse logo, at an unknown Plymouth location.

BAYLY'S SERPOLLET

Richard Bayly bought one of the first cars in Plymouth when he was a young man in his early twenties. Son of the Robert Bayly, who owned a long-established timber business in Plymouth, Richard purchased a Gardener Serpollet steam car which he appears to have run for but a little while. Like his brother, John, Richard was a keen early motorist and could afford to try different machines.

In 1905 he bought a 28hp Mercedes but he hadn't had it long when he decided he'd like to upgrade to a 40hp Mercedes. The price would appear to have been around £1,500, a considerable amount of money then and somewhere around £180,000 today. However the Bayly family were among the most affluent in the area at that time and Richard's father had only relatively recently (1882) rebuilt the imposing family home at Tor (now a home for the blind at the top of Hartley).

In a strange sequence of events leading up a court case in January 1906, before the new, more powerful Mercedes had even been delivered, Richard, allegedly, informed his supplier that actually he'd rather have a six-cylinder Napier.

Mr Hutton, whose company was the one tasked with ordering the new Mercedes and disposing of the original, was unhappy because they were selling the second Mercedes on commission only, and couldn't get anything like what they were anticipating for the sale of the first vehicle.

Questions over who owed what to whom, and how much, led to the affair being heard in court before Mr Justice Darling. Hutton alleged that the first car was not delivered in perfect condition and that they 'would not take your body'. To which Mr Justice Darling responded, much to the court's amusement, that the proper remedy for that would be Habeas Corpus.

Meanwhile, in the course of the hearing, it transpired that the speed indicator of the old motor car was to be transferred to the new one. Here we must remember that the automobile industry was still in its infancy as Mr Justice Darling said: 'I see in a letter it is stated that speed-indicators are absolutely useless.'

Again there was laughter in the court.

Speaking on behalf of Mr Hutton, a solicitor called Disturnal replied that speed-indicators 'are supposed to indicate the speed, and motorists require them for their protection.'

Justice Darling was clearly enjoying himself and regarding the matter of speed-indicators said 'I sometimes think it would be useful if they were marked "Manslaughter, fines and imprisonment", a suggestion that was, once again, followed by "loud laughter".'

Darling raised another titter when he said: 'These cars are made in Germany, aren't they, like most things?'

At the end of the day it transpired that the original Mercedes had been sold for £700 and that that money had been paid into court with the proviso that the sum would go to whichever side won the case. Bayly's solicitor 'pointed out to the jury that there were tricks in horse-dealing and tricks in motor car dealing.'

The jury found for the plaintiff – Richard Bayly was that winner.

A 1903 Gardener Serpollet and contemporary advertisements.

TWO WHEELS GOOD THREE WHEELS BETTER?

In 1885 Carl Friedrich Benz filed a patent for what was widely considered to be the world's first practical motor car to be put into production. Twelve years earlier the young German engineer, then in his late-twenties, had developed a successful petrol-driven piston engine and thereafter focused on finessing a fully motorised vehicle. The first incarnation of this was the Benz Patent-Motorwagen, a motorised tricycle with a rear-mounted engine. The machine featured many innovations of Benz's. It was constructed of steel tubing with steel spoked wheels and rubber tyres.

On 3 July 1886 Benz unveiled his motor vehicle in Mannheim and thereafter kept applying for regular patents to reflect the various refinements he was making along the way.

Quite early in this process his wife, Bertha, decided, in August 1888, to drive two of her sons to her home town on a Benz Patent-Motorwagen No3. The 66-mile journey was a great success. Hailed as the world's first ever long distance car journey, the event is celebrated every other year in Germany with a vintage car rally.

Unvelied internationally at the 1889 World's Trade Fair in Paris, around 25 Model III machines were made, and over the next ten years a further 572 Benz vehicles were produced, making them the most successful car manufacturer in the world at that time.

Top: Children on a tricycle next to Sherwell Church c1900.
Above: c1895 A tricycle parked in Bedford Street with the Globe Hotel in the distance. Right: A Benz Patent Motorwagen of 1888.

HENRY STURMEY'S AUTOCAR

Henry Sturmey and his Autocar.

In the afternoon of 19 October 1897 Henry Sturmey arrived at Land's End in his recently acquired four-horse-power auto-car. Over the course of the previous few weeks he had driven his English made Daimler down from John O'Groats, completing the 926 mile drive at an average speed of 10 miles per hour. The journey was widely reported across the country, as it had been the first lengthy test of a motor car in the United Kingdom. Much was made of the fact that Mr Sturmey himself weighed in at around 15 stone, and his servant-cum-travelling companion, Richard Ashley, 11 stone, and they had nearly 200 pounds of baggage and oil supplies – this making all the more impressive the fact that the car had managed to cross the Ord of Caithness, the Grampian Mountains, to Ullswater, over the Kirkstone Pass down into Ambleside and via the 'extremely hilly country between Exeter and Bodmin' without a hitch.

'The autocar,' noted 40-year-old Sturmey, 'was working better at the finish than at the beginning of the journey.' The motor car was very much a novelty at that time, it was almost certainly the first to be seen in Devon and Cornwall and the public at large were still somewhat sceptical about the machine.

Sturmey was keen to point out that it 'steers as easily as a bicycle, is absolutely under control at all speeds, can be stopped in ten feet, and cannot by any possibility run away,' and 'that both vibration and smell are entirely absent when the car is running, that but little, if any, more noise is made than by the hoofs of a pair of horses on a hard road, and that the car, which is seated for five persons, is most comfortable to ride in, travelling steadily and evenly at all speeds without any of the jolting or swaying movements usually conveyed to a carriage by the action of the horse.'

The consumption of oil, or benzoline, was reckoned at 114 gallons, which averaged out a cost of three-farthings a mile. Having reached his destination he started out on his return journey to Coventry, where he was based, via Helston, Falmouth and Truro, his intention being to travel along the south coast.

Sturmey was at that time the editor of the newly instituted *Autocar* magazine, a role he was easily suited to having already been founding editor of *The Cyclist* magazine for the last ten years and of the *Photography* magazine since 1889.

Indeed he'd combined these two interests a couple of years earlier when he'd hosted 'lantern social' at the Royal Assembly Rooms in Leamington and given a talk 'illustrated with photographic slides' about his cycling tour through North Italy and Switzerland, to the South Warwickshire Cyclist Club.

Having been born in Somerset and started out in life as a schoolmaster, his career had taken an interesting turn after publishing the first edition of the *Bicyclist's Handbook* in 1877. An early director of Daimler and the short lived Great Horseless Carriage Company, he was one of the country's great early advocates of the motor car and worked on their design, engines and gearing – his name was long remembered for the Sturmey-Archer three-speed hub gear patented in 1900.

Later that year a nasty accident sustained while testing an experimental car saw him stand down as editor of *Autocar*, but his interest in the industry continued and in 1907 Sturmey Motors manufactured light vans, before he became interested in taxicabs and commercial vehicles.

Sturmey died, unmarried, aged 73, at his Coventry home, in 1930.

Henry Sturmey, left, with Richard Ashley and Mr E W Newton who'd joined them in Camborne. Sturmey had ordered his car at the end of 1896 and took delivery of it in September 1897. He had just one lesson before embarking on his epic John O'Groats to Land's End drive later that month.

DRIVING ROUND THE BENZ

No sooner had Henry Sturmey completed his epic cross country adventure than we found him lining up for the Motor Car Club's first anniversary event of the great Emancipation Run from London to Brighton. Commemorating the elimination of the Red Flag Act that decreed that no self-powered vehicle be permitted to use the road without a flag-bearing pedestrian leading the way, the anniversary event was staged by the Motor Car Club in November 1897. The President, and co-founder of the club was 45-year-old Harry Lawson, a celebrated bicycle designer, racing cyclist and motoring pioneer.

Allegedly Messrs Tope and Rugg Monk at Yealmpton c1906 outside Mother Hubbard's Cottage, the driver however looks rather like Francis Pearse, who claims to have driven Plymouth's first car. The car looks rather like his Benz, so the date would be about right as Pearse registered his car in 1907 and as we see here the car has yet to be given a registration number.

In 1896 he founded the Daimler Motor Company in London, having bought the right to use the name Gottlieb Daimler and the German Daimler-Motoren-Geselllschaft company. That same year he organised the Emancipation Run and was a leading light in the advancement of the new transport. The whole ethos of the MCC was 'for the protection, encouragement and development of the motor-car industry.'

'Its members,' read a contemporary report in the *Morning Post*, 'are animated by a profound belief in the future of the motorcar, and yesterday they spared no pains to give the public an object-lesson in what has already been accomplished.'

Mindful of potential critics, the Motor Car Club was keen to point out that 'In this country the motor industry is only 12 months old.' The implication being that teething troubles were inevitable.

Several hundred guests were invited to the anniversary bash and 'the rendezvous for the cars was at Whitehall-place, outside the Hotel Metropole, and that the public were interested in the event was shown by the fact that long before the appointed hour of departure crowds began to assemble. Special police arrangements had been made, and thousands of people lined the route in the vicinity of Whitehall, Trafalgar-square, Cockspur-street, and Pall-mall.

'The number of motors that assembled to traverse the appointed route from Whitehall to the Sheen House Club, Richmond-park, was 39. They were of many shapes, sizes, and designs. One or two had steam for their motive power, others had oil, and electricity made a goodly show, including an example of the electrical cabs which Londoners have recently seen plying for hire in the streets, and which certainly seem to have attained no small measure of popularity. Lawson's own machine was 'a handsome coupe, painted yellow and black, known as the Rothschild car, the cost of which has been set down at 1,000 guineas.

'This vehicle, given a clear roadway, can be run at a rate of 25 miles per hour, and is said to be capable of attaining a speed of 30 miles, and as the Committee of the Motor Club put it: "it is equally efficient for visiting purposes or long journeys, such as London to Brighton or London to Birmingham".'

Henry Sturmey's recently-designed Daimler, was 'a conspicuous figure amid the array of motors, and the other types included open and closed carriages, waggonettes and a nondescript vehicle which appeared to be a compromise between a small omnibus and a baker's van.'

One notable difference 'in connection with the departure generally was that the vehicles moved off with much less clatter and noise than was apparent a year ago. Something has been done to diminish vibration in motors since last year, and the pervading odour of oil was not so potent as on the occasion of the first meet. In the matter of noise the worst offenders are the motor cycles, and while in the case of the larger motors there is a good deal of panting and snorting while the motive power is being got ready, the noise is not obtrusive once a start has been made: and the vehicle can be made to run both smoothly and swiftly.' Furthermore it was noted that 'in one or two types a good rate of speed reduces the pulsation and sound to a minimum.'

The route taken by the procession on this occasion was not as demanding as the run to Brighton and the route to Sheen House was only about eight miles ... 'and the smartest of the motors covered it in about 40 minutes.

'The police had made admirable arrangements, and while throughout the greater part of the route there were crowds of sightseers the way was well kept without any inconvenience to the ordinary traffic. The drivers of horse-drawn cabs and omnibuses indulged in the usual "chaff" at the expense of the motors, and cabby's general attitude appeared to be that of treating the horseless carriages as rather a good joke. As for the horses, their attitude for the most part was one of complete indifference, though the obtrusive clatter of the motor cycles was resented by some of them. On Barnes-common the unusual spectacle induced a horse yoked in a butcher's cart to bolt, but the procession arrived safely at the Sheen House Club without accident and, it may be added, without incident.

'At the club luncheon was served, and the guests were afterwards shown a demonstration of motor cycle riding on the club's track. Mr. Charles Jarrott, on a motor bicycle, rode two miles in 5min. $24^{1}/_{5}$ sec, and some fast riding was accomplished on a tricycle by Mr. F. T. Bidlake. There was no organised procession back to town, but most of the cars returned by the original route, their progress through the streets being observed by many thousands of spectators. It may be added that while many of the cars run were of foreign origin as regards their invention, they were all of British manufacture.

'In the evening the members of the Motor Car Club dined together in the Whitehall Rooms, Hotel Metropole.

Two men, possibly Mr Tope again, with maybe a Mr Pasqua, a Greek food importer, in 1908 pictured in Downderry. The car is a 1900 8hp Napier.

Top: 'Photograph of a man with his new c1903 6hp model Q De Dion Bolton on the Barbican. Bottom: Mr Irwin gives Mr Trethewey a ride beside the Drill Hall, Saltash, in his new c1906 Phoenix Quadcar.

'Mr. Henry J. Lawson, President, was in the chair, and about 150 ladies and gentlemen were present, the company including the Earl of Fingall, Lord Norreys, the Hon. E. S. Rolls, Major Wingfield, the Mayor and Mayoress of Richmond, and Messrs. B. B. Van Praagh, H. Times, A. J. Walter, W. W. Beaumont, and Jerome K. Jerome. The President, in giving the toast of "The Motor-car Industry," referred with gratification to the fact that his Royal Highness the Duke of York had honoured the Motor Car Club by becoming one of its members. (Applause.)

'Referring to the criticisms to which the pioneers of the motor-car industry had been subjected, he said that they were regarded as being too revolutionary, but in this respect they were in good company. The promoters of the first railways had to live down similar criticism, and it was 10 years before the London and North-Western Railway Company could get their first Bill passed.

'By means of the motor-car it was possible for people to go short journeys, such as that from London to Richmond, more quickly, more cheaply, and more conveniently than by railway. (Hear, hear.)

'He believed that half the time of the world was wasted in waiting for trains, which, after all, generally took people to points which were some distance away from the places they wanted to go to. In his opinion every town at the present time needed the convenience of electric cabs. The prospect before the motor-car industry was so enormous that he believed motor-car factories would have to be set up before long all over the country. He thought it would be admitted by all unprejudiced observers that great progress had been made during the last 12 months. In the British-made motor-car every defect which was apparent in the cars of a year ago had, to a very great extent, been minimised. Every year would see a further march forward, so that one might as well try to prevent the flight of time as to stop the progress of the new industry. (Applause.) The people of to-day would a few years hence laugh at the state of things which existed in 1897, when men and women walked so much and the slow people punished the fast people by actually making speed an offence.'

Dr W H Waterfield's Benz, one of 29 vehicles registered locally in 1908, although the car is older than that. In the days when Doctors drove to patients who could afford their services, cars were a very useful and, generally, efficient way to get around. This horseless carriage is substantially made of wood, the high driving position is a throw back to the days of horse-drawn carts and enabled the driver to see over the horse, while the wooden board to which the registration plate is affixed is another legacy of the horse age as this was to stop the driver being 'dashed' by stones thrown up by the horse's hooves – hence dashboard.

PLYMOUTH'S FIRST MOTOR CAR

Francis Pearse in his 1901 Benz.

chose the quietest one we saw – a 4¹/₂ horse-power Benz.' With its engine 'of horizontal pattern' and mounted at the back of the machine, the car, which boasted a 'Victoria body' was built in Mannheim, Germany, and Mr Pearse apparently paid £240 for the green machine (around £30,000 in today's terms). 'We drove back to Plymouth in it, and it was the only car we saw on the road,' recalled the self-styled, "happy bachelor".'

Describing the vehicle in some detail Mr Pearse noted that: 'the gearing comprised three speeds, forward and reverse and was fitted with solid tyres. It also was equipped with seven lamps and two horns, one operated by bellows beneath the car, with a strident-voiced whistle "for couples".'

Francis Henry Pearse was born in Plymouth in 1871, his father, and his two uncles and his grandfather were all doctors, each of his two younger brothers would become doctors, but Francis was destined to be different – he was to become a dentist ... and the first owner of a motor car in Plymouth.

With a keen sense of fun and adventure, he looked back on the world from a personal perspective in the summer of 1938 noting how his grandfather, Dr William Pearse, had gone around his practice in Launceston, visiting his patients on horseback, while his father, Dr Thomas Pearse, 'recognising the march of progress' had attached a cart to the horse.

Francis was a young man of 30 when he and his brother went to London to buy his petrol-driven pioneering vehicle in 1901: 'We

Being the first car in the Three Towns, the Benz inevitably turned heads wherever it went.

'Fear was the chief emotion provoked,' recalled Mr Pearse, reflecting on the furore his motorcar generated. Not altogether surprising perhaps when its driver 'knocked down a man in Union Street and ran over his leg.' Fortunately for both parties it was a wooden leg!

A contemporary report in the *Western Daily Mercury* from 20 August 1901 saw an inspired journalist comment that he found travelling through Plympton and district in Mr Pearse's car at pace of twelve miles an hour 'decidedly novel and exhilarating.' He further admitted, 'rather ruefully,' ... 'that the occasional application of the brake was "sufficiently sudden to be disconcerting".'

Years later, in a newspaper interview in 1938 the intrepid dentist noted the difference between his day and his grandfather's day was that 'in these days of fast travelling one can drive, without undue effort, from London to Exeter in seven hours,' while in 1822, around the time his grandfather achieved his medical qualification, 'an enterprising coach proprietor was advertising "London to Exeter in Thirty-Six Hours".'

And according to a contemporary Georgian poster in the possession of Mr Pearse: 'From thence goods are immediately forwarded by John Woolcott's light fly wagons to run to and from Plymouth, Dock (Devonport), Falmouth, and all parts of Devon and Cornwall and complete their journeys in half their former time.'

A great change then from a century or so earlier, but thereafter change was not so slow, although, a decade later, there still weren't many cars on our roads and in 1912 Francis Pearse challenged a fellow motoring enthusiast, Richard Cooke to a motor race over a course 'from Drake Circus, through Brixton and Yealmpton to Newton Ferrers.'

Conducted under the auspices of the Marble Molar Automobile Club (remember Pearse was a dentist) the 'Rules for Competitors' included the following: 'Engines must not be changed en route; The track being a single one, an over-taking car is not allowed to jump over its predecessor; Competitors must cover the course on 20 gallons of petrol and one soda and milk; Competitors are allowed to push their cars ... and tin-tacks, broken bottles, sardine tins, and jam jars must not be thrown in front of the foremost car.'

By all accounts their adventures were not unlike those in a Charlie Chaplin film: 'Mr Cooke developed engine trouble at the start and Mr Pearse maintained the lead to Billacombe, where he found the contents of the cylinder water-jacket in a boiling state, and being absorbed into the cylinder itself. The fire-buckets at the station were utilized, but the delay of 35 minutes enabled the competing machine to get ahead. Later, Mr Pearse and his companion, by getting out and pushing the car up a hill, actually overtook their opponents! Thus the cars passed and re-passed and Mr Cooke eventually won by a minute or so.'

The irrepressible ivory carpenter Pearse, subsequently immortalized the occasion in thirteen verses, and maintained a long-standing protest against the decision!

Francis Pearse was in many respects as much of an exhibitionist as an orthodontist. Three years before purchasing his Benz he had had a 'cruise' across London in a hot air balloon with Captain Percival Spencer, one of the celebrated family of British aeronauts who had then recently completed a number of cross Channel flights.

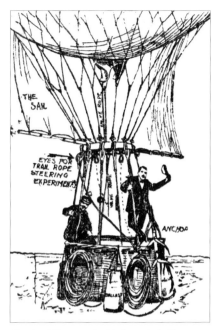

Percival Spencer in his hot air balloon.

On Saturday 2 April 1921, in protest against an increased tax on motor cars, Francis stripped the engine off the frame and contrived to insert a bicycle frame to power the vehicle thereby creating a motor car upon which he could not be taxed (the increase was from £1 carriage tax to a £9 annual motor tax). Appearing with his contrivance in Old Town Street, Pearse caused quite a stir and became the 'centre of interest to hundreds of people and the police had to turn out in force to keep the public on the move as he was not going fast enough to keep up with their walking pace.

'With the assistance of a gang of enthusiastic youngsters, Mr Pearse pedalled a laborious way up the hill, the bizarre effect being increased by the fact that he was bareheaded and that the mechanics was so constructed that he had to revolve the bicycle cranks backwards in order to go forward. General consensus was that it was a late April Fool stunt, but it wasn't.

Followed by a reporter into a small back lane garage (Pearse lived in Queen Anne Terrace) the journalist stated that he spent a most interesting half-hour with Mr Pearse 'who was gasping out of breath after his violent exertions.'

"I could never have done it," averred the exhausted tooth extractor, "if I had not practised for the last twenty two nights up this side lane. The machine weighs half a ton. It's a silent protest against the increased tax on cars," he explained.

Curiously enough, many years later, in January 1939, Pearse met Captain George Eyston, who had twice set world speed records. A former motorcycle racer and twice winner of the French Grand Prix in the 1920s, Eyston broke the 100 mph barrier in 1933, but four years later set a new land speed record of 312 mph in his Thunderbolt, a speed he increased to 345 mph the following year. Remarkably that record was quickly eclipsed by John Cobb, but Eyston kept up the rivalry. However, when he met our Francis Pearse at the 1939 Shell Mex exhibition in the Guildhall, the local man claimed that this was a unique coming together of the fastest man on earth with the slowest, as his Benz had been going at less than one mile an hour back in 1921.

The engine wasn't gone long though and in 1928 Pearse entered his car with engine back in London to Brighton, Emancipation Day Run between London and Brighton. The term 'Emancipation' refers to freedom from the earlier legislation whereby a man with a red flag had to precede each vehicle on the road.

It was a popular event among the owners of older cars and Pearse's Benz was to participate in the race three more times in the 1930s.

But sitting proudly atop his treasured green motor wasn't the Devon dental surgeon's only way of attracting attention. At 12.30 pm, on Wednesday 9 October 1929, the 58-year-old Pearse, having spotted steeplejack's ladders on the church spire opposite his house in Queen Anne Terrace, successfully mounted an attempt on the 150-ft Sherwell Chapel Steeple 'without permission.'

'He performed the feat with remarkable agility and once at the top blew a whistle which he had taken with him in order to attract the attention of the passers-by in the adjoining thoroughfare and released a number of paper streamers, which floated from the spire right across the street. Owing to the boisterous weather which prevailed he was unable to fix his flag to the top of the spire, as he had hoped to do but upon returning to earth he expressed himself as highly pleased with his performance.'

Asked why he undertook the climb, Dr Pearse explained that there were two reasons: First of all because he was challenged to do it for a shilling, and, secondly, because someone had alleged such an ascent was a good cure for certain bodily ills. In view of his profession he felt it his duty to ascertain whether the remedy was a good specific for the malady mentioned.

Dr Pearse confessed that he had not sought permission to make the ascent but felt that nobody would object to his little escapade which went to prove that 'a man is as old as he feels.' Several friends congratulated Dr Pearse on his achievement, and among them was the challenger, who willingly paid over the shilling which had been responsible for the climb being undertaken.

The ascent was also witnessed by an official witness, Mr J Jerritt, who professed that in his opinion 'it was the nearest point to heaven that Francis Henry Pearse will ever attain.'

That itself was interesting as it was the second time he had performed the feat, the first being 'many years earlier', when weather conditions were more favourable.

The last local chapter in the saga of Mr Pearse's Benz is, like all things associated with our Mr Pearse, a convoluted one. The story broke with our tooth sayer writing to the *Western Morning News* on 12 March 1931 complaining that the iron roof that had sheltered his precious vehicle from the rain for the previous 30 years had now been given a £5 rating assessment which meant that henceforth he would have to pay £2.10.0d (around £175 in today's terms) a year 'for the pleasure of keeping Plymouth's first motor car, which is used now very occasionally, and then only to advertise the name of Plymouth far and wide.'

Mr Pearse had, he said, 'letters from persons in Canada, Australia and New Zealand who have had the name of our city and its old car mentioned in their newspapers'– the Commonwealth was still a big deal in those days!

His missive continued: 'As the accommodation is not suitable for a modern car, the roof will have to be taken down. It goes against the grain to sell my dear old car as a whole or in parts. I have therefore very reluctantly decided to bury it and have already been making arrangements to find a site where a pit can be dug, and Plymouth will then see the last of its first car forever.'

Five days later, another letter, this time from J Jerritt (the witness to Pearse's Sherwell Spire ascent) ran thus: 'Many of the local inhabitants will be sorry to learn that the worthy owner of the well-known old Benz has definitely decided to commit it to the grave.

'It is a strange coincidence that since the unsympathetic Assessment Committee taxed the apology for a garage to shelter the poor old Benz to such an exorbitant figure the engine has absolutely refused to function. It is, however, gratifying to learn that a suitable site for the burial has been selected, not in the Old Cemetery, but near-by, where a full "derelict" service will be held and "Last Post" sounded as a final act.'

All very melodramatic, and creating quite a stir as it was reported in the local press on 23 March 1931 that as a result of the story being made public Mr Pearse had received 'sympathetic inquiries and some definite offers for the car as a curio.

'Letters and telegrams have descended upon Mr Pearse until, as he says: "my head is in a whirl, and I feel I ought to engage a staff of secretaries to deal with the matter".'

There then appeared a list of over 50 locations from which correspondence had been received, from Basingstoke to Brockenhurst and Broadstairs to Beaulieu.

At the same time it became apparent that he had offered the car to Plymouth Museum but the museum committee didn't feel they had the space, it wasn't the first car in the country just the first in Plymouth and anyway Pearse didn't want to give it to the museum merely loan it for display and he wanted to reserve the right to take it from time to time.

However, there was no escaping the fact that he had received good offers for the car and while, in his own words the car 'may be a bit stale to the present generation, but future generations will have different opinions; they will regret its loss.'

For their part the Museum said they would be glad to accept the car on condition Mr Pearse allowed it to be sent to the City of Hull Museum of Transport.

In the event the car was sold, for £35 (around £2.5k today) to Cecil Burney of Brooklands, Weybridge, to the Motor Museum there. Brooklands had been constructed as the world's first purpose-built motor racing track 25 years earlier and had cost its local landowner, Hugh Locke-King, his personal fortune (around £16 million in today's terms).

Ethel Locke-King leads the opening parade at Brooklands in 1907. Inset: Poster for a 1924 event at Brooklands.

Francis Henry Pearse drives his beloved green Benz to Friary Station, on its last local outing, Friday 17 April 1931.

It's interesting to note that it was dubbed the 'Motor Ascot' initially by the press and in the beginning a number of the procedures were steeped in the equine racing culture. Cars were brought together in the 'paddock', shod with tyres, and weighed by the 'Clerk of Scales' for handicapping. Meanwhile drivers were asked to identify themselves by wearing coloured silks, like horse racing jockeys.

But before it could reach Surrey the Benz had to leave Plymouth. Driving it to the train station at Friary was not an option as if the car were to be driven Mr Pearse would have had to take out a road licence, driver's licence, and the third party risk insurance and so he proposed to push it instead: 'Dressed in frock-coat, tight-fitting light tweed trousers, and silk hat, Mr Pearse sat at the steering wheel of his ancient car as it travelled on its own volition downhill on its way to Friary Station. A small party gathered to raise a cheer as the Benz started on its last run in Plymouth. Along the level ground in Ebrington Street, however, the method of locomotion was different. Willing schoolboys readily lent a hand in pushing the car along, while Mr Pearse still maintained his position on the driving seat. Just to show that the old vehicle was still capable of 'going through its paces' nicely, Mr Pearse filled the tank with petrol after the vehicle had got on to the Southern Railway Company's private road at Friary and with a couple of swings at the fly-wheel, situated by the engine at the rear of the car, started it up. It went around the private roads with remarkable speed and climbed the incline towards St Jude's Church, and then in neutral gear returned along Beaumont Road to its starting place. Some of Mr Pearse's friends then made a short trip in the car around the goods yard and subsequently as a farewell to his car Mr Pearse produced a bottle of ale, and after filling a tumbler proceeded to toast his old friend.

'He waited to see the Benz hoisted on to the platform ready for entraining, and, with a last, long look, left the station to return home. "It's like parting with an old friend, but it is my intention now to go for a cruise to the Mediterranean to try and forget it. It will be my first holiday for nearly 40 years".'

Post Script

Intriguingly a question mark hangs over what happened next – did the car ever reach Brooklands, was that actually its final destination? In 1938 the *Western Morning News* reported that the Benz was one of 14 vehicles from 1901 entered in the 1938 London to Brighton run, and that it was entered by a J Bradshaw and driven by a Mr R Seaman.

The name Bradshaw rather than Burney came up again when a clause in Pearse's will contained the dentist's express wish that the car be bought from its present owners for a sum not above £100 and presented to Bristol Museum. According to the *Lancashire Evening Post*, of 20 December 1947 Mr Ewart Bradshaw, of Preston, 'the owner', said that he was 'reluctant to part with the car, as it completes my collection, which dates back to 1896.

'It is, he added, in perfect condition and has taken part in most London-Brighton runs in recent years. I don't see why Bristol should have it, instead of Preston, and at the moment I can't dream of letting it go.'

The report then noted that: 'Mr Bradshaw bought the car from Mr Pearse 15 years ago for "between £80 and £90." Curiously enough though, when speaking to the *Western Morning News* a couple of days later, Mr H Bradshaw – the governing director of Messrs Loxham's Garages, in Preston, told the paper that he bought the car from Mr Pearse 15 years ago, and that he paid more than £100 for it originally. If that was true, that would have meant that the Brooklands story was not true and that our Mr Pearse pocketed three times more than the £35 he claimed!

Most odd, particularly as Pearse was clearly not short of money, as evidenced from the account of his estate as reported in the *Lincolnshire Echo* of December 1947, it evidently amounted to £13,126 (net personally £12,604, that is around £.5million today).' The paper further reported that 'after legacies of £250, Mr Francis Henry Pearse, a dental surgeon of Queen Anne Terrace, Plymouth, left the residue "to the State of the Realm absolutely for the relief of the national debt of this my country".'

PLYMOUTH'S FIRST FEMALE CAR OWNERS? MRS WETHERBY WILLIAM

Elizabeth Wetherby-Williams was an intriguing woman. In the January 1912 edition of the *Illustrated London News* she was photographed in her 12-20-hp Humber in the grounds of her home, Little Efford, on the edge of Plymouth. She evidently claimed to have named her motor 'The Silent Satisfaction' on account of 'its smooth and silent running' and professed to have clocked up about 90,000 miles since 1904. 'A gallon of petrol carries it about 24 miles,' read the text, 'and the shock-absorbers effect a great saving to the back tyres.'

It appears that Thomas and Elizabeth Wetherby-Williams had arrived in the neighbourhood some six years earlier, setting up home at Widey Court, and inviting the great and the good of the area to garden parties there. Mr WW was an engineer and the grandson of an extremely wealthy Welsh copper mine proprietor who had expanded his interests into Cornwall, while Mrs WW said she was descended from a lowland Scottish family 'connected to the Stuarts'.

Elizabeth's maiden name was Erskine, and the couple named their eldest daughter, Margaret, and as Margaret Erskine (which as it happens was the same name as the Scots King James V's favourite mistress), their daughter would go on to write a large number of crime/mystery novels. She specialised, according to one critic in 'eccentric British families with long-held secrets, social pretensions, and heads of households with streaks of cunning' adding the disparaging rider that 'she wrote the same book ... twenty one times.' All titles featured the same leading character – Inspector Septimus Finch.

One suspects that young Margaret did not have to look too far for inspiration. Her parents were not at Widey Court for more than a few years (the property, now long-gone, had associations with Charles I, the Stuart king). However they were at the well-appointed Little Efford house for an even shorter spell as Thomas WW put the property up for sale in May 1912.

The following month they appear to be resident in 3 Marine Parade in Dover. Then, a few years later, just after the end of the Great War, we find them living in Mount Pleasant, in Ilfracombe, and then West Usher ... and then Broadstairs.

In 1935 Mrs WW now with just her two daughters, bought a 'somewhat grim-looking' Georgian mansion, Walters Hall, at Monketon-in-Thanet, near Ramsgate. A local builder was commissioned to do the place up and before long the grand home had been reinvented as 'Walters Hall Country Club'.

Locals were surprised that such a venture should open in such a remote spot, but Mrs WW began to make contact with officers stationed at Manston Royal Air Force base a mile or so away. To add to the attractions of the bar that had been installed, Mrs

"My car never goes wrong, costs practically nothing for upkeep, is easy on the tyres and on our hilly Devonshire roads, and averages 18 to 20 miles to the gallon of petrol. As you know, I have driven the car entirely myself during the whole of the time." So claimed Elizabeth Wetherby Williams. She also claimed to have had the car since 1904, however the number plate looks like CO 513 which wasn't until around the time the Illustrated London News *item appeared, but perhaps it was CO 50.*

Widey Court.

WW engaged 'six beautiful young women as dancing partners. The hostess also came to an arrangement with local garage proprietors to send out cars and cabs to ferry young RAF officers to and from the club (the Wetherby-Williams' only son, Arthur had served in the RAF during the First World War and in 1919 was, apparently, according to *The Aeroplane* due to marry Helene Sonia de Stomph, only child of his late Excellency General Baron Antonie de Stomph and Baronne Sophie de Stomph nee Comtesse Zyndram Kovstialkovsky).

One day at Walters Hall Country Club, however, after an apparent loss of lighting at the house, Mrs WW and her two daughters 'most mysteriously disappeared.'

A report in the *John Bull* magazine observed that 'When Mrs Wetherby-Williams arrived at Monkton-in-Thanet she created the impression that she was a woman of considerable means, and boasted that she had wealthy connections abroad. Now she has disappeared and her mansion of mystery is deserted.'

Twelve months later and giving her address as The Mound, Dorchester, Elizabeth arrived in Detroit, Michigan, with her now 38-year-old son, Arthur. On his paperwork Arthur said he was looking to take up permanent residence in the United States, and certainly he died on the other side of the Atlantic in the early 1960s. Elizabeth meanwhile evidently moved back to Britain and the last sighting we could find had her in Bexhill on Sea elected to the committee of the local Literature and Drama Group, in 1946. Doubtless she had many tales to tell!

MRS MARIE AUGUSTA DALTON

Born in the USA, in 1878, Marie Augusta Dalton was in her late twenties when, in the summer of 1906 she was charged with 'furiously driving a motor car' on Derriford Hill.

Evidence was given by George Partridge of Crownhill who stated that he noticed that the car, a Sunbeam, was going at the rate of 30 miles an hour. Frederick Dawe, a coachman, affirmed that the vehicle was 'not going at a reasonable pace'. Local postman, Frederick Sparrow, said that the car was going very fast – 'about 20-25 miles an hour.' Meanwhile the opinion of Police Constable Osborne was that 'the car was going at a tremendous speed.' Mrs Dalton herself claimed that 'my brakes went wrong and it took me sometime before I could right them'. Quite how anyone back then had anything like an accurate idea of the vehicle's velocity when motors were such a rare sight – there were barely 80 cars/vans/lorries registered across the Three Towns – is a matter for conjecture and certainly after hearing the evidence of Mr F Davis (presumably the very same RF Davis who had a garage in Crownhill, one of the first garages in the wider area), the Bench dismissed the case, 'considering the evidence insufficient.'

Curiously enough Mrs Dalton was soon in the news again, this time as 'the other woman' in a divorce case between Mrs Manuelo George Alice Blackburn (nee Stubbs) and her estranged husband, Arthur Blackburn of the Hayne Estate, Devon.

In a story that made the *News of the World*, the 'matronly-looking' Mrs Blackburn had not lived with Mr Blackburn since receiving knowledge of his conduct back in 1885. Clearly those were different circumstances but there was little doubt now that he was spending considerable time with the aforementioned Mrs Dalton, of Braeside, Wilderness Road, and that the couple appeared to have children together. A Judicial Separation was granted.

Later that same year Mrs Dalton was in the news yet again, as her cook's man friend, a labourer, Percy Philip Turner of St Jude's was given two month's hard labour for stealing a diamond ring from Mrs D's bedside. Interestingly enough R Rugg Monk (mentioned earlier in this book) was one of the magistrates who heard the case.

DUGGUA & SONS Est. 1864

George Randolph Duggua went to sea as a ship's mate while in his teens. Born in Plymouth in 1864, he went to Jago's School, in Cobourg Street, and lived with his parents, Roger and Elizabeth, in Raleigh Street. His parents were both Cornish and they apparently moved to Plymouth just before George was born – his older sister, had been born on the other side of the Tamar. In the same year that George was born his father appears to have set up as an iron merchant in 20 Raleigh Street and the family lived above the premises.

Roger had been a master mariner himself and indeed was employed as such when he and Elizabeth were married, in Liverpool, in 1848.

Roger also owned his own boat, or boats, and in the early 1890s, in addition to manufacturing all manner of things metallic, they also proudly advertised the fact that they 'held in their warehouses large stocks of bar iron, sheets and plates, lead, nails, tin plates, and all general requirements too numerous to detail, for ship builders, engineers, and general iron trades, builders, ironmongers, etc, each of the leading lines being conducted in separate departments, not the least important of which is that of

1907 Duggua Brothers ad. Top left: 1894 sketch of Raleigh Street premises.

galvanizing, they being the only firm conducting this branch of trade west of Bristol.'

They were also advertising 'the largest stock of roller skates in the district' and happy to state that they had 'all makes'. But more than that even they were among the pioneering cycle agents in the area. Indeed they claimed the distinction of 'being patronized by three-fourths of the cycling community of the Three Towns.' 'The extent of space covered by the whole of the premises is very considerable, and far more so than an inspection of the Raleigh Street front shop would lead the visitor to believe.'

Like so many of the early cycle dealers in town it wasn't long before they embraced first the motor cycle and then the motor car. By that time the business was in the hands of the brothers, as Roger had died in November 1899 at the age of 77.

It meant he missed the dawn of the new century and the arrival of motor cars in their showrooms. By the summer of 1902 and now operating as the Duggua Brothers, rather than Duggua & Sons, they were advertising a 3¹/₂ horse power Benz, not new, but in good condition and working order. Certainly it couldn't have been that old!

A couple of years later they were publicizing their latest range of Centaur motor cycles: 'chain or belt driven … superb machines.' They were also offering practical repairs and petrol, and this was well before the advent of the petrol station.

In 1905, his youngest brother James Montrose, died, aged just 36, the business nevertheless continued as Duggua Brothers and they were still advertising as engineers and motor trade supply stores in 1915. But it would appear that George retired soon after that and by 1919 he had retired to live in Hartley, in Greystone, Bainbridge Avenue, which was then in Compton Gifford, just outside Plymouth. His brother William died in 1931, but George survived until December 1949 when he took leave of the world at the ripe old age of 95, his wife, Florence, just a few weeks later.

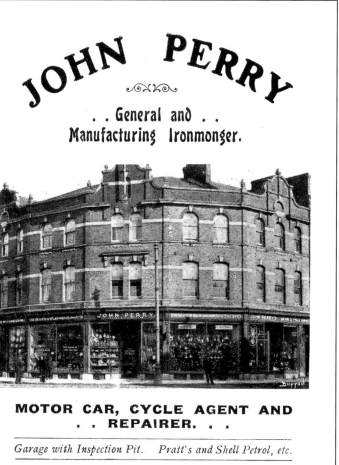

1910 advertisement for one of Stonehouse's Motor Car agents.

Spooner's Corner (at the bottom of Old Town Street) c1900 before the fire of 1902 devastated the block behind the tram. Note the Spooner's sign on the flat wall. Chubb's Hotel is the next building.

WILLIAM HEATH PLYMOUTH'S FIRST MOTORIST?

An article published in the *Western Morning News* on Tuesday 30 December 1947 suggests that William Heath, of Prince Rock, was the first person to drive a motor vehicle in Plymouth.
Mr Heath claimed that he was driving a Daimler motor van for Messrs Spooners in Plymouth in 1897.
Heath explained that he went to London in November, 1897, to collect the van, a twin cylinder, tube ignition, tiller steering, chain-driven Daimler, from a dealer's at Chiswell Street, near the Bank. Shortly afterwards William said that he drove the van from London to Plymouth along the coastal road via Bournemouth and Bridport.
'I set out with a member of the motor company on a Friday morning,' said Mr Heath, 'thinking that the journey would be completed in a day. I chose the coastal route because I thought I would give the vehicle a thorough test, but we had many breakdowns, on occasions having to push the van up hills. We stayed the night at Bournemouth.
'On Saturday we encountered the same trouble, the van would not take the hills and we finally arrived in Plymouth at 8 o'clock on Sunday evening.'
The journey had taken them 35 hours and 15 minutes!
'I particularly remember it because people were coming from St Andrew's Church as we reached Chubb's Hotel in Old Town Street and hundreds gathered round to stare with amazement at the van.'
One of the first people to be driven in the van in Plymouth was a *Western Morning News* reporter, who was taken across the plains of Mutley, near Townsend Farm, and up Townsend Hill. Despite alterations to the sprocket wheels, which created a great deal of improvement, it was found that the van could not compete with

the hilly countryside of Plymouth and in March, 1898, it was returned to London.
The van had been used, however, for advertising purposes and the delivery of parcels and other goods for the firm. After the return of the Daimler, Mr Heath said he drove a Riley van for the firm, which was replaced about 12 months later by a Willys Overland which proved to be the best van of all.
William Heath retired from Messrs Spooners, aged 71, in 1941 after 51 years service with the firm.
The piece concluded by stating that at the time of his retirement William Heath was driving a Leyland furniture removal van.
So without wanting to doubt Mr Heath, the issue remains, this was a van, not a car, and so what we have here maybe the first petrol-driven vehicle in Plymouth, but it wasn't a private car, so is Francis Pearse's vehicle still worthy of that claim?

Above: A later Spooners' van c1925, was this another one that William Heath drove? Right: An 1897 ad for Spooners, then one of the biggest businesses in the Three Towns.

Sydney Parker at the wheel of his Colliers van, an Albion perhaps, in the middle of the road at Yealmpton, outside Mother Hubbard's cottage – note the wording on the front – Driver takes Orders. Right: Sydney's driving licence from 1910.

SYDNEY PARKER
MOTOR CAR DRIVER

Plymouth born and bred, 90-year-old Fernley Parker, says that his father drove a very early vehicle for Colliers in Plymouth and it had solid tyres, no windscreen, carbide lamp headlights and a hand honked horn.

Sydney Thomas Parker was born in 1890 to Thomas and Emily Parker, when his parents were living in King Street. His father died when Sydney was still in his teens and the family moved to Belmont Street.

There were no driving tests in those days but under the terms of the 1903 Motor Car Act all drivers had at least to have a licence to be on the road and Fernley has a collection of his father's driving licences, the first of which was issued in 1910, which certainly makes him one of the earliest drivers in town. Although Sydney didn't have his own vehicle, his stated occupation from age 21 at least, was Motor Car Driver. In the photograph he's the one at the steering wheel, and the lad next to him appears to have had a variety of uses, not just with deliveries, but Fernley recalls one of his father's stories about how Sydney was out on the moors on the road from Horrabridge, coming up to Yelverton, on a particularly dark and foggy afternoon. Sydney suggested that the lad with him at the time should jump down from the vehicle and walk ahead to make sure they could keep the vehicle on the road. The lad, by all accounts, was almost paralysed with fear, and disappeared into the fog, and soon afterwards Sydney and the van found themselves off road, in one of the gardens of the houses on the left as you approach Yelverton from the west.

Married on Christmas Day 1912, Sydney drove for a number of different people and companies, including a scrap merchant in Flora Street who clearly did extremely well for himself. Indeed one day, having ordered a new Rolls Royce Silver, the scrap man sent Sydney up the line to pick up the vehicle.

However when he got to the showroom, the salesman not would let Sydney drive the car away because Sydney hadn't passed the Rolls Royce drivers test ... he hadn't even been aware that there was such a thing. The boss was contacted by telephone.

His response was somewhat blunt. 'What's all this about a bloody test, if my man can't drive the car you can stuff it and the deal's off.'

Sydney drove the car home. The boss was an earthy character, Fernley doesn't think that he drove himself, which was probably just as well as he was 'drunk as a hand cart most of the time.' Another one of Sydney's acquaintances who was fond of a drink, was 'Uncle' Dick – he wasn't a real uncle says Fernley, you just called a lot of the people your parents knew uncle or aunty. Anyway, Dick worked with Sydney at the Starkey, Knight and Ford brewery. Sydney drove vans and Dick went out with a dray horse and cart. Often on making a delivery to a pub the landlord would offer the drayman a half a pint, which Dick would readily accept. One time he got so drunk that he fell asleep at the reins. Fortunately the horse knew the route well and delivered Dick back to base. Sydney recalled the horse nudging the door with his nose while Dick was snoring like a train on the cart! Some will recall all manner of roundsmen with their horses and carts and be familiar with some horse who knew exactly where to stop for a delivery before they were pulled up by the driver. Makes one marvel at the concept of vehicles that didn't need drivers all those years ago!

During the Great War, Sydney signed up as a driver and spent most of his war years in France driving Army lorries.

Curiously enough in the Second World War, for part of the war effort, he had to drive his company lorry, which was requisitioned by the Government, up country and just leave it in a muddy field with loads of others. For a man who'd always meticulously maintained his vehicles it was an unhappy moment. Back in the First World War, Sydney used to take the spark plugs out of an engine to stop it freezing up in the night, and sometimes, when it was particularly cold, he would sleep under the engine.

The new Co-op grocery van, St Michael Avenue, Keyham c1903.

THE CO-OP AND THE HORSE

By January 1907 the Plymouth Co-operative Society had more horse power than ever before – hence the decision to build an all-new stable block at Peverell, adjoining their bakery there.

It wasn't just a question of delivering produce from the abattoir, bakery, boot factory, farm or warehouse to one or other of their many outlets either. To meet the demand from members where there was no handy Co-op shop or just to provide a regular service for different neighbourhoods, door-to-door dairy and bakery, delivery vans had already been operating for some years.

Then, in March 1903, the Society had introduced a new service – the horse-drawn greengrocery van. The first of these vehicles was designed by joiner and builder, John Spry of Station Road, Devonport and orders were instantly placed with him for even larger models. By the end of the year the greengrocery department already had twelve such vans on the road and a further four were on order, in anticipation of being required.

Significantly at the beginning of that year there was no such thing as the Plymouth Co-operative greengrocery department, its earlier incarnation had simply been the 'Potato Department'. The change reflected the Society's increasing growing capacity across their extended farmlands and market garden facilities.

The move also led to another new initiative: on 30 December that year, 1903, the Society acquired a sizeable freehold property off Sutton Road, Coxside, that they might relocate the Works Department from their now quite cramped quarters in Week Street. Eighteen months later they moved the Firewood Factory from Devonport to the new Alma Yard site at Coxside and around the same time decided to establish a wheelwright and coachbuilding section.

Why pay someone else to manufacture your carts and carriages when you had the wherewithal to do it yourself?

The greengrocery delivery van operation was, however, still small beer when compared to the dairy department, which, around this time, was serving around 12,000 families in the Three Towns each day. When you consider the average family size around that time that would have represented a significant percentage of the local population – comfortably somewhere between a quarter and a third.

Some 68 Co-op milkmen were, between them, responsible for the deliveries, each with an average of 172 families on each of their rounds.

The milk was apparently delivered daily in sealed churns to the dairy shops – from local farms and then, after inspection, poured into churns on the delivery carts for door to door selling. This would be done by the milkman ladling the milk into a measuring jug and then ladling the same into the customers' own jug or container – with rarely a bottle in sight!

Often greengrocery or dairy vans would have a roundsman and a boy working the round. Young lads, fourteen or younger (with parental consent) would knock on doors and take orders while the roundsman stayed with cart, partly to prevent pilfering and partly to stop the horse going off on his own, although most of the milk was delivered on hand barrows. Some of the grocery branches also employed boys to deliver weekly parcels to anyone living within a reasonable distance – this way the Society was able to reach further and further afield with each branch that opened.

One must assume that delivery boys were also using bicycles, for the ironmongery department were selling them in 1907; guaranteed for five years, with best quality tyres and two-rim brakes – yours for £5.

In the summer of 1908 there was an exciting new development as the Society road-tested its first horse-less carriage – a steam wagon – supplied by Robey & Co. of Lincoln, registration number FE 443. Purporting to be capable of carrying a five-ton load, the wagon was severely tested in its first month. Attempting to transport five tons of building materials to the Society's farm at Wiverton, the motor was strained and required costly repairs. Thereafter the capacity was capped at four tons – much to the frustration of the committee.

As the 1920s dawned the Society had decided that hiring road transport no longer made good sense and so started buying up a variety of vehicles of their own.

This too had its down side: 'Our first haphazard system of having all kinds of machines' was soon 'replaced by a gradual standardisation on two or three reliable types of machines, with spare parts in stock.' This meant that 'a speedy repair in case of temporary breakdown could be effected by our own engineering staff at the garage on North Quay.'

W J Lapthorn, writing in 1920, then added: 'A very important adjunct of this department is the "Char-a-banc" which provides for the recreation of our vast membership during the spring and summer seasons, and keeps the prices at reasonable limits and enables our membership to see the beauties of nature in two or three counties of the South West of England famous for its natural beauty as well as being a profit for the Society.'

All this was not to suggest that the age of the horse was over, far from it, horse-drawn door-to-door delivery vans 'are as essential now as ever' and at the end of the war the number of working horses had actually increased 'in the aggregate', to 135, with another 80 in service on the farms.

An outing of charabancs, Guildhall Square photographed from St Andrew's Church tower.
Top right: A Co-operative charabanc outing in what was officially termed a hackney carriage - it was permitted to travel no faster than 12 mph - note solid tyres and cobbled road surface.

However, the indications were clear and in a paper produced for the 'First Co-operative Trades and Business Conferences' in 1921, R W Royle, the traffic manager for the Co-operative Wholesale Society, wrote: 'A comparison of the merits of the motor vehicle as against the horse-drawn vehicle would obviously lie in favour of the former under certain conditions.'

He then added: 'It is impossible to make a general comparison between horse and motor on account of the fact that horses could not travel the distances easily covered by motors, but there are still some instances where the horse can retain its usefulness with economy.

'The capital cost of the horse and its vehicle may be anything up to £200, in addition to which there is the wage of the driver; but in the case of the motor vehicle, the cost may be upwards of £1,000 and in addition there are the wages of both the driver and his mate. As the wages of the motor driver alone exceed those of the driver of the horse lorry, it is obvious that not only is more capital standing idle, but that a great wages bill is accruing.'

Maintenance was another time-consuming issue with these early motors: 'If on return of a vehicle to the garage at the end of the day, the vehicle shows signs of requiring mechanical adjustment, it should have attention immediately and not be left until the morning, as time must be given each morning for a general look over the chassis. Strict attention must be paid to lubrication. Efficient lubrication is the key to success in the running of a motor vehicle, and the garage foreman, or whoever may be in charge, should see that this is carried out.'

There was also the issue of fuel and a storage tank for petrol was considered 'an essential instalment of every (Co-operative) garage. 'It is a very good practice to insist on the tanks of all vehicles being filled immediately after the day's work, so that the drivers are left free next morning to attend to the starting of their engines.'

In terms of design and location Royle suggested that 'the garage should be as near the commencement and termination of the day's work as possible. There should be an entrance and exit at opposite ends of the building so as to obviate any necessity for reversing and turning vehicles in the garage, which only means lost time and occasional accidents.

'Plenty of headroom and natural light are essential. If artificial light is needed a number of small lights over the gangways between the vehicles are much better than a few big lamps, which only throw shadows.'

Co-op vehicles outside their garage facility on North Quay, Barbican.

Top: Andrew's taxi ... a Manchester made Belsize
Above: Humm's taxi ... a c.1910 Unic?
Left: Humm's charges as they appeared on a postcard.

"TAXI" SIR?

For many people their first direct experience of sitting in a motor car would perhaps have been a ride in a taxi cab.

As early as 1901 we read of 'the intention to start a motor-car service between Plymouth and Plympton.'

'It is instructive,' read the report, 'to have the opinion of the Right Hon Henry Chaplin [a senior politician and celebrated race horse owner], that there was no reason why an average speed of 20 or 25 miles an hour on an open road might not be permitted. 'He is strongly convinced of the possibilities of the motor-car, and of its usefulness as a means of transit, and would safeguard the public by requiring certificates of efficiency from drivers of motors licensed to run at a speed of over 12 miles an hour, and demanding that the cars should be fully capable of identification. 'This question of automobiles has more than a passing interest for Exeter, for opponents of a tram-line through High-street ask, "Why not a motor service for congested towns?"

'Advocates of the electric system would probably reply, 'Because they would most likely add to the congestion.'

The piece is interesting as it is a little ambiguous as to whether we're talking motor cars rather than tram cars, or buses rather than trams. Either way the ascendency of both was inevitable given their ease of getting around and not needing a rail network. It would appear that Plymouth's first taxi cab in the current understanding of the term was a vehicle built by William Mumford on the chassis of a model T Ford. The taxi was then sold to Jack Andrew of Andrew's Garage.

A clear contemporary of H (Jack) Andrew, was Robert Humm whose early advertising in that direction was uncannily similar, however it would appear that Humm, and quite possibly Andrew, were operating in not fully charted waters.

London-born Robert Humm arrived in Plymouth as a teenager in the late 1880s and by the early 1890s had established a business

EARLY MOTORS & MOTORISTS

selling and repairing all the major makes of bicycles. Something of a pioneer in the booming cycle trade locally, he was one of only a dozen or so operators in the Three Towns at the end of the nineteenth century.

By 1910 he appears to have taken over Walter Williams motoring operation in Old Town Street and there he lived above the showrooms with his wife, four sons, four daughters and two teenage servants.

In February 1912 we find him in court in what was virtually a test case in the debate about 'plying for hire.' Magistrates were asked to settle the issue under the Plymouth, Stonehouse and Devonport Carriages and Boats Act of 1877.

One of Humm's drivers, Fred Smith, had been summoned for having driven a taxicab without a licence. Percy T Pearce was the prosecuting solicitor and describing the case as one of 'considerable importance,' he said that in recent years there had been brought into use what were commonly known as taxicabs. 'In order that the interests of the public might be properly looked after, the Legislature had created bodies in the various districts to control the persons plying for hire in the street.

'Pearce explained the steps the local Commissioners under the Act took to safeguard the public using the taxicabs, and proceeded to intimate that Smith had previously held a licence from the Commissioners, and was thus conversant with the steps that ought be taken.

'Smith left the employ of that particular firm and joined Mr. Humm. On November 8th officials of Mr. Gard, clerk to the Commissioners, and three others, Mr. Lovelace and PCs Somers and Honey, saw a taxicab outside Mr Humm's garage. Smith, who was the driver, said the car was for hire, and drove the men to Millbay station, where he received a shilling. It transpired that neither Smith nor Mr. Humm had a license as required by the Commissioners.'

'James Knight, managing clerk to the clerk of the Commissioners, affirmed this to be true, whereupon the defence lawyer Mr. Elliot Square asked; "Is there a single motor-car or taxicab driver in Plymouth. Devonport, or Stonehouse who is licensed to drive except those employed by the Provincial Motor Cab Company?'

"I know of none," said Knight.

"And there are a large number of taxicab owners?"

"Yes."

Square proceeded to point out that the Provincial Motor Cab Company's taxicabs, which stood on the hackney carriage stands, and their drivers were licensed, but such was not the case with other taxicabs or drivers in Plymouth.

'Yet no proceedings had been taken against the latter persons for not being licensed. In nearly every case the taxicabs were engaged by means of the telephone, and, therefore they did not ply for hire. On the day in question Mr. Humm's taxicab was outside the garage for convenience, and the driver was about to take it inside, owing to a shower, when Mr. Knight engaged it. It was not necessary for the taxicab to be licensed by the Commissioners, for it did not ply for hire in the streets, stand on the ranks, or pick up casual customers, every engagement having to made through the office at the garage.'

Humm was sworn in and stated that he had given instructions to each taxicab driver that he was only to fulfil engagements made through the office at the garage. He was not present when Mr Knight engaged the cab.

The Magistrates' Clerk then asked: "You don't allow any of your drivers to pick up passengers in the street?"

"No fares are picked up unless they come to the garage."

A legal argument ensued about he question of plying for hire, and at the conclusion the magistrates consulted together. Eventually they came to the conclusion that the taxicab was let for hire by Smith without a licence, and he would be fined one shilling (the amount he had charged for the journey) plus costs. Meanwhile the case against Robert Humm was dismissed.

Clearly this had been something of a set up, as intimated by the presence of the two police constables, but presumably the outcome hadn't been quite what the Commissioners were hoping for, as it appears to have condoned the existing practices in the area.

View from the Dockyard gates, a Ford Model T of c1915 passing Agnes Weston's Royal Sailor's Rest on the corner of Fore Street and Edinburgh Road.

EARLY FORD OWNERS

Ken Hawke's father bought his Ford (above) in 1916. He says that the picture was taken in 1918, when the car was permitted to be run under the Defence of the Realm Acts (DORA). 'It shows my father (Francis Hawke) holding my brother, also Francis, then aged two, plus our mother and other family members.
'The car was sold on the closure of father's business on 13 June 1918, just before he joined HM Forces – it fetched £155.
'My father had a garage and taxi business at Greenbank and, at that time, also had horse-drawn cabs. The car was regularly used for weddings, the bride would travel in the car and the guests would go by horse and cart.
'Father had his first driving licence (signed by the then Chief Constable) in 1912. Father also had one of the early petrol pumps in Plymouth, he had it installed in the front garden of our house in Greenbank Terrace around 1921. Eventually we bought the garage across the road, which was formerly Pooley's Bakery.
'Father's first car was bought from Kimber's Garage in Albert Road, Devonport and over 50 years later, in partnership with Ivan Lang and his brother Ron, we purchased Kimber's Garage and renamed it Lang's Garage.'

'I purchased my first new motor car in 1919,' wrote the eminent local chemist Fernley Wallis in his reminiscences (published in 1965). It was a Ford Model T (pictured above) and cost £220. Petrol was 3/- a gallon. There were no 30 mph limits, no controlled streets, such as one-way traffic. You could cross anywhere provided you kept to the left-hand side. The number of cars was infinitesimal; policemen were on point-duty at the busy spots, Ebrington Street Corner, the top of Treville Street, St Andrew's Cross, and the top of Union Street.'

Top left: 1918 Baby you can drive my car – two-year-old Francis Hawke at the wheel of his father's Model T Ford, CO 1642, registered in 1916. Top right: Fernely Wallis's Model T CO 2470 Above: Cundy's Model T pick up

LOCAL REGISTRATIONS
1904-1936

How strange it seems that the year that Plymouth Argyle went fully professional, an act was passed requiring all motor cars to be registered and given a licence plate and that the first car to be thus registered after 1 January 1904 with a Plymouth plate, CO 1 was a 16/20 hp Argyll, made in Glasgow.

Here's a wonderful image that, to be honest, we don't know much about. We don't know who these people are, where the photograph was taken, or when it was taken. Not a promising start, except that the start banner itself may well give someone else a clue.

My best guess on this one is that it was taken sometime around 1924 and it was some sort of vintage car event, even back then. The reason for this is partly the way the ladies are dressed – they look far more Edwardian than post-Great War, Roaring Twenties, and the car. The car is remarkable, perhaps not for the make, a 1904 Argyll, but for the registration plate – CO 1.

That rather special number plate suggests that while this may not have been the first car to have been seen on the streets of Plymouth it was almost certainly the first car to have been registered.

Plymouth's somewhat eccentric dentist, Francis Pearse, consistently claimed to have been the first car owner in the area back in 1901, but he didn't actually register his machine until 1907, three or four years after CO 1 was issued in 1904. By the end of that year a grand total of 18 vehicles had been registered in Plymouth, with a further ten in neighbouring Devonport, each one sporting the other local prefix – DR.

After the initial rush had subsided it appears that only 13 vehicles were registered the following year in Plymouth and a meagre seven in Devonport. Thereafter, however, the numbers went in one direction only, up. In Plymouth 19 vehicles were registered in 1906, 11 in Devonport, then 23 and 12 respectively in 1907, when Pearse acquired his CO 53 plate.

Even then all the cars on the road in the area would barely have filled any of major car parks.

By the time war was declared in 1914 there were over a thousand cars registered locally and, despite the difficulties endured during wartime, by the end of the Great War in 1918 the number had grown to over 3,000.

Curiously enough, however, Devonport (DR) registrations were temporarily halted in 1915, the last one being DR 268 and it was not until 1926 that DR 269 was issued. It should be remembered that the Three Towns, Plymouth, Devonport and Stonehouse had been amalgamated towards the end of 1914 and doubtless this was the reason for that move.

DR then became the wider Plymouth prefix as CO 9999 had been registered that same year and there appears to have been no appetite for a five number sequence.

The licensing authorities then issued DR plates until 1932 when DR 9999 was issued, at which point a new prefix was introduced for the City – JY.

It's illuminating to reflect that while it took from 1904 to 1926 (22 years) for the first 10,000 vehicles to be registered locally, it only took six years, 1926 to 1932 for the second 10,000 vehicles to be registered here, such was the rapid rate of increase in petrol-driven vehicles across the country – although doubtless a disproportionate number of those in the early days were motorbikes.

And how long was it before all of the 9,999 JY numbers had been issued? Just five years! Small wonder that vehicle showrooms, dealerships, garages and countless other related enterprises had sprung up in the meantime. The petrol-driven vehicle was clearly here to stay, at least for the foreseeable future.

Approximate issues of Plymouth vehicle registration numbers at start of each year						
CO - Plymouth and Stonehouse			DR - Devonport			
YEAR	From - To	Qty	From - To	Qty	Total	
1904	CO1 -18	18	DR1 - 10	10	18	
1905	19 -31	13	11 - 17	7	20	
1906	32 - 50	19	18 - 29	11	30	
1907	51 - 73	23	30 - 42	12	35	
1908	74 -102	29	43 - 57	14	43	
1909	103 -136	34	58 - 75	17	51	
1910	137 - 176	40	76 - 96	20	60	
1911	177 - 233	57	97 - 121	24	81	
1912	234 - 321	88	122 - 152	30	176	
1913	322 - 523	202	153 - 191	38	240	
1914	524 -820	297	192 - 235	43	340	
1915	821 - 1225	405	DR236 - 268	32	437	
1916	1226 - 1684	459	temp. halted			
1917	1685 - 2156	472				
1918	2157 - 2648	492				
1919	2649 - 3168	520				
1920	3169 - 3749	581				
1921	3750 - 4424	675				
1922	4425 - 5292	868				
1923	5293 -6307	1015				
1924	6308 - 7514	1207				
1925	7515 - 9356	1842				
1926	CO9357 - 9999	643				
1926	DR269 - 1183	1915				
1927	1184 - 2834	1651				
1928	2835 - 4501	1667				
1929	4502 - 6164	1663				
1930	6165 - 7855	1691				
1931	7856 - 9520	1665				
1932	DR9521 - 9999	478				
1932	JY1 - 1135	1614				
1933	1136 - 2780	1645				
1934	2781 - 4827	2047				
1935	4828 - 7272	2445				
1936	JY7273 - 9545	2273				

Ready for an outing, an assembly of cars on the Barbican's cobbled Parade c1924.

MAJOR STRODE, NEWNHAM

Among the founding members of the Devon Automobile Club was Major George Sydney Strode Strode. The second son of Admiral Arthur Lowe he had assumed the Strode surname in 1897 when, aged 36, he inherited the family estate of Newnham Park.

An eminent freemason, he was made Provincial Grand Master in 1904 and was appointed Sheriff of Devon by King Edward VII in 1906.

A local magistrate and alderman of Devon County Council, as a Vice-President of the Devon Automobile Club in 1907 he expressed the view at a meeting of the club in October 1907 that 'we should bring the greatest possible pressure upon the County Council that the Devonshire roads and lanes were not the safest places for driving.'

As a later chairman of the Devon County Roads Committee he was well placed to deal with the issue.

The photographs here feature his 1906 Argyll motor car.

Above: Outside Newnham. Opposite page; A welcome break or an unwelcome break down? Note the horse and trap heading towards them.

WILLIAM TEGLIO

With a base in Commercial Road and waterside premises on Commercial Wharf, was the Italian wine-importing business of the Teglio brothers. Given the popularity of wine this country today it is difficult to appreciate the lengths that Messrs Teglio & Co had to go to in the 1890s to sell wine here. They were, after all, the first to supply genuine Italian wines in the West Country and in the publicity material that accompanied one their early promotional pieces they were eager to point out that on account of their 'wholesomeness and purity the wines of Italy are highly recommended by medical faculty.'

Indeed after detailed descriptions of the wines themselves the advertisement concluded with a quote from the medical journal *The Lancet* which described wine generally (as long as it was not artificially sweetened) as being 'a beverage of great utility as a stimulant, and which does the very minimum of harm.' Then it added: 'A population that drinks only wine rarely produces a dipsomaniac.'

William Teglio in his 1907 Hotchkiss Type L, with wife Jane, son Max and daughter Norah. Max was then at Kelly College – he would later die in France in 1917 in the Great War.

ARTHUR POLE PENTON

In 1914, Major-General Arthur Pole Penton (General Officer Commanding, Plymouth Defences) declared that, in the event of an emergency he didn't want messengers frantically cycling off to the Mayor of Plymouth, the Mayor of Devonport and the Chairman of the Stonehouse Council seeking consensus on something requiring an instant decision.

War looked entirely inevitable at that point in time and Parliament agreed with the military man and 'The Local Government Provisional Order Bill for the unifying of the Three Towns' (Plymouth, Stonehouse & Devonport) was eventually passed despite a feisty campaign by the Devonport authorities to stop it. The campaign was still raging weeks after war had begun! The idea though was nothing new, it had been discussed by the then newly formed Plymouth Chamber of Commerce back in 1814 and had been reconsidered by various bodies in the years in between. However the people of Devonport were right to be concerned and the decision was to have profound consequences.

WILLIAM BOOTH

Born in 1829, the same year as the woman destined to become his wife and soulmate, Catherine Mumford, William Booth was a methodist preacher and, together with Catherine, was the founder of the Salvation Army in 1865. In time he became known as 'General' Booth and Catherine was dubbed the 'Mother of the the Salvation Army.'

In 1909, aged 80, William Booth, set off on what was already his sixth motor tour of England. Two years earlier he'd toured America and the following year he would campaign in the Netherlands, Denmark, Germany, Switzerland and Italy, before embarking on his seventh and final motor tour of England. Famously he would preach to assembled crowds from the back of his open topped tourer.

Celebrated as one of the largest distributors of humanitarian aid of all time, it is said that Booth used a variety of makes of motor car and they were invariably painted white and had red wheels, the colours reflecting those of the Salvation Army shield.

1914, 'Slightly wounded Highlanders having a joy ride to the Hospital, and they certainly looked as if they were enjoying it. General Penton, in charge of Plymouth Fortress, is on the left of the picture.' Caption from Doidges Annual, the car is a new BSA 10 with a sleeve valve engine.

General William Booth (with the white beard in the back) setting off for Plymouth in his powerful 60hp white Darracq (he had also had an Enfield and a Renault).

OTHER EARLY CARS SEEN HERE

ROLLS ROYCE IN THE DOCKYARD

The photograph of this November 1924 20hp Rolls Royce is interesting because it sports a 'Spirit of Ecstasy' figurine above the radiator.

Ornaments surmounting radiators had become something of a fashion among Rolls Royce owners and in 1909 Lord Montagu of Beaulieu, a celebrated motoring enthusiast, commissioned his friend, the sculptor Charles Robinson Sykes, to create just such a thing. Lord Montagu was then enjoying a passionate affair with Eleanor Velasco Thornton and she became the model for Sykes's piece, leaning forward in fluttering robes, with a finger on her lips to symbolise the secrecy of the love affair.

In 1910, by which time many owners were producing their own, often 'inappropriate' radiator ornaments, Claude Johnson, the then managing director of Rolls Royce was tasked with commissioning a suitable generic mascot. Sykes was approached and he came up with a variant of what had been dubbed 'The Whisperer' and that was the now iconic 'Spirit of Ecstasy.'

1917 Wellsbourne House: Mr and Mrs William B Snell of Wellsbourne House, Hartley Avenue, Compton, Plymouth, together with motoring friends organising expeditions for recuperating servicemen. This was one of many ways in which local well-to-do people felt that they could help spread a little happiness during the 1914-18 war. Nancy Astor was another mover and skaker in this field.

A Buick of c1914 outside a distinctive Plymstock residence.

A chauffeur-driven 20hp 1924 Rolls Royce in Devonport Dockyard.

JACK MEW
THE PRINCE'S DRIVER

Liz Reardon's grandfather William James (Jack) Mew drove the Prince of Wales during his tour of the city in 1931.

On 15 July Jack drove the Prince from Princess Square to the dockyard to visit HMS *Nautilus*, to the local hospital fair and to Roborough to officially open Plymouth's new airport. The heir to the throne had been due to fly down to the airport but the weather wasn't good enough.

It was by no means the first time Mr Mew had chauffeured a celebrity and it wouldn't be the last. Among those Jack had in the back of one vehicle or another were Lord St Levan, Earl Fortescue, the Earl of Morley, Viscount and Viscountess Astor, the Earl and Countess of Mount Edgcumbe, the Earl of St Germans, many members of Parliament, King George VI and Queen Elizabeth and Emily Pankhurst.

Jack Mew was is in charge of the fleet of hire cars operated by Messrs Humms, of Princess Square and at that time he had already been with Humms for 32 years. He had joined the firm as a mechanic back in 1899 and his driving career with the company started in 1917, when Jack was 32. However, despite averaging around 20,000-25,000 miles a year in the job, the 1931 occasion was the first time he'd chauffeured a member of the royal family. 'You can imagine my pleasure when I heard that I had been chosen to drive the Prince,' he said in a local press interview at the time. 'It was certainly an experience driving through the cheering

This page: Jack Mew in the driving seat of Humm's Sunbeam limousine, with the Prince of Wales and Plymouth's Mayor, Clifford Tozer, in the back.

crowds – and having a clear road all the way. I didn't feel the slightest bit nervous.'

Jack's interview gives us something of the flavour of the early days of motoring in Plymouth.

Indeed one of his first jobs was to help Robert Humm to construct the first motor-cycle ever seen in the city.

'This motor-cycle was used at Home Park, where they used to run motor-cycle races in those days on a hard, banked track,' he recalled, adding: 'I remember a French man who raced on a tricycle there. It was not so thrilling as dirt-track racing but we thought it wonderful in those days.'

Another of his earliest memories was working on the first Sunbeam car ever to arrive in Plymouth, which was sold to Mrs Dalton of Mannamead, a candidate for being Plymouth's first woman driver.

'Motoring,' continued Jack in his reminiscences, 'used to be a hazardous business in the early times and breakdowns were frequent. One of the greatest troubles was running out of petrol.' Remember ... there were no petrol gauges on cars back then!

'I remember once finding the tank empty when driving between Liskeard and Lostwithiel,' recalled Jack. 'There were no petrol stations, of course, and after we had been held up an hour we were thinking of persuading a farmer to drive into Lostwithiel for some petrol when a motor dealer from Bodmin happened to drive by.

'Although it was only six o'clock in the evening, this was a most unusual and extremely fortunate occurrence – for one could drive for hours in those days without meeting another car – and the dealer was able to spare us a drop of petrol to get as far as Liskeard.'

Another of Jack's stories conjures up yet another remarkable insight into those early days:

'I remember doing a non-stop journey to London and back in 1908. We left Plymouth at 9.30 on a Saturday evening and returned at 10 o'clock on Monday morning. You could shave 12 hours off that journey today.'

With a fair wind and relatively clear road you could do it in a lot less today, even though there is so much more traffic on the road. Among the first people to see the possibilities opened up by the car were the politicians. It enabled them to get around and see a lot of constituents in a much shorter period of time.

'One of the first Parliamentary candidates to use motor-cars for his election tours was Mr Isaac Foot, whom I drove for a fortnight during the General Election of 1910, when he unsuccessfully contested Totnes Division. Later in the same campaign I drove the late Mr 'Tommy' Agar-Robartes in the South-East Cornwall division.'

Remarkably, during the whole of his driving career, at least up until 1931, Jack Mew never had an accident. His recipe was always 'safety first' and he believed that most accidents were caused by drivers taking risks.

The Prince with the Mayor, Deputy-Mayor, and Town Clerk arriving at Plymouth Municipal Aerodrome on 15 July 1931 – note the Humm's Sunbeam RD 5266 on the left.

The Queen of Romania accepts a bouquet from a young girl in Fore Street, Devonport, May 1924.

THE QUEEN OF ROMANIA
31 MAY 1924

With Waldorf Astor, outside the Astor residence - 3 Eliot Terrace.

Princess Marie Alexandra Victoria was the eldest daughter of Prince Alfred, the Duke of Edinburgh, and granddaughter of Queen Victoria. In the early 1890s, when her father was Commander-in-Chief locally and based at Mount Wise, the teenage princess spent a couple of happy years here and was ever willing to make return visits.

In 1893 the 17-year old princess married Prince Ferdinand of Romania, ten years her senior. The couple had six children, three boys, three girls, although the relationship was not a particularly happy one and there were suggestions that one or two of the children were sired by other men, one of them by an Astor. Marie was very friendly with Waldorf Astor, before he married Nancy and came to Plymouth as a prospective MP, and her friendship with the family was to be enduring.

In 1914, following the death of her husband's uncle, Marie became Queen of Romania, although because of the Great War they were not properly crowned King and Queen until 1922. In her capacity as the Romanian Queen, Marie made a number of visits to Plymouth, like the one captured here, 31 May 1924. On her visit to Plymouth and Devonport, she was accompanied by her sister, Princess Beatrice (officially Princess Alfonso, Infanta of Spain), and her brother-in-law Prince Alfonso of Spain.

The Queen's tour took in Plymouth Guildhall, The Hoe, Devonport Dockyard and the Alexandra Maternity Home, Stoke.

The Queen of Romania visits Plymouth in 1924 in an open top Rolls Royce. Note the early pneumatic tyres on the London-registered Rolls Royce transporting the Queen, and the early AA badge on the grill, but no Spirit of Ecstasy. Note also the line of Royal Marines holding the crowds back.

Nancy Astor on the campaign trail in 1919 in a horse and carriage

THE WHEELS OF POLITICS

One thing most political candidates like to do in the run up to an election is to be seen – and heard – by as many potential voters as possible. In the age before radio, television and the internet, that meant travelling around as much of the constituency as possible, and in the days before the motor car that meant with a horse and carriage, or on horseback or on shank's pony (for younger readers that means to rely on one's own shanks, or legs, this is, to go on foot).

Of course, not everyone had access to wheeled transport, however in the nineteenth century and earlier, most potential politicians were 'well-heeled', in other words they were quite well off and not 'down at heel'. They were not reliant on old boots or shoes that were well worn, and they could afford to travel around in a carriage.

Certainly there are famous images of the country's first female to take her seat in the House of Commons, actively campaigning from inside an open carriage.

In 1919 when Nancy Astor decided to contest the seat that her husband had held since 1910 (and which he had to give up when he agreed to inherit his late father's title and sit in the House of Lords), she made good and conspicuous use of that mode of transport. She also made use of a motor car.

Nancy and Waldorf Astor were, at that time, one of the wealthiest couples in Britain, notwithstanding the King and Queen. Furthermore as a newspaper proprietor (he had acquired *The Observer* from his father in 1915), Waldorf knew the power of a good press photograph and so some stunning images were taken of Nancy on the campaign trail.

Undoubtedly one of the most memorable of these was taken addressing a large crowd in behind a complex of Barbican properties, underneath a long line of washing.

Nancy Astor sets out her stall from the back of a car at the rear of a local housing complex, possibly around Nicholl's Court behind Notte Street where a new housing development would be built in the late 1930s and which would be opened by Lady Astor herself. Note how almost everyone is wearing a hat!

Nancy canvassing outside the Cattle Market Inn, opposite the old market and behind Old Town Street, Plymouth.

It's interesting to note, however, that the Astors were by no means the first politicians to deploy the motor car in an election campaign.

Barely two years after the first petrol-driven motor car had been seen in this country James Tuke, of Harrogate and the Yorkshire Motor Company, drove the Liberal candidate for Bradford South Ward, Joseph Dawson, around the constituency. The date was 31 October 1896, while the vehicle was his Arnold motor carriage (Walter Arnold, of East Peckham, Kent, was the first person in the UK to have a concession for Benz cars – it was an Arnold Benz that won the first ever London to Brighton run).

Dawson, who had been on the council for some years already, was able to use the vehicle as a platform for open-air meetings. Then, on polling day, 2 November, Tuke allowed the car to be used to take voters to the polls. The hope, clearly, was that they would be boosting the Liberal vote in this way, but Tuke wasn't convinced that all those who were thus transported were true supporters. 'Many got their first ride in a motor car under false pretences' he later observed.

As it transpired Dawson polled 26 fewer votes than his Conservative rival. Meanwhile, in 1919 Nancy Astor polled more than 5,000 votes more than her nearest rival, indeed she polled more votes than the two other candidates put together.

William Gay, the Labour candidate, came second while bringing up the rear was a man whose son would one day be a local MP, and who would serve for Bodmin, Isaac Foot.

Isaac was elected as a Liberal councillor in Plymouth in 1907 and served for two decades, during which time he presented himself as a parliamentary candidate several times (Totnes in 1910, then a couple of times at Bodmin, then Plymouth in 1919, before eventually being elected at a by-election in Bodmin in 1922. He retained the seat in a second election held that year, and again the following year. Beaten in Bodmin 1924, he regained the constituency in 1929 and held it through to 1935).

Standing next to Isaac Foot, on his left, is the then Mayor of

Top: Nancy Astor victorious, in a Wolseley, outside Plymouth Municipal building. Bottom: Waldorf Astor, William Gay, Nancy Astor, Colonel Guest, Town Clerk, Isaac Foot, Lovell Dunstan (Mayor).

Plymouth, Lovell Dunstan. Dunstan was a successful local politician who, in 1923 took control of the Conservative party. 'He was a ship chandler', wrote Crispin Gill, who, 'from a little room behind his shop in Southside Street ... ran Plymouth. 'Callers there would find him there with one or more of his cabal, all businessmen: GP Holmes, WJW Modely, FD Baxter, WHJ Priest – all chairmen of the major committees.'

Top: Isaac Foot with supporters and his Cornish registered vehicle. Bottom: Lovell Dunstan c1924 (in a new Humber 8 Chummy) and his local campaign team.

Of course motor cars weren't the only mode of transport available in early twentieth century election campaigns and on the opposite page here we see two of Arthur Benn's supporters on an early BSA motorcycle. One can but wonder how long the Benn's Our Man poster stood up to the wind as the lads made their way around town.

The motorbike was registered in 1924. This was a time when BSA's core business was fading. The Birmingham Small Arms Company had started out back in 1861 in the Gun Quarter of Birmingham, as a military and sporting firearms company, but had diversified into bicycles (in the 1880s), motorcycles (in 1905), then cars (Daimlers), buses and various hand power and machine tools.

During the Great War their focus shifted back to arms production, notably Lewis Automatic quick firing machine guns, but by 1924 there was little demand for firearms and most of their profits were coming from car and motorcycle manufacture. 1924 was also the year of Sir Arthur Shirley Benn's last successful election campaign in Plymouth. He triumphed over two local men, Labour's Jimmy Moses and the 1924 Liberal Mayor, Solomon Stephens. Five years later Alderman Jimmy Moses, a dockyard shipwright and Methodist lay preacher, would turn the tables on Benn and win the seat.

Born in Ireland in 1858, the son of a vicar, Benn was educated at Clifton College, Bristol, and enjoyed a successful career that saw him appointed as British Vice-Consul to Mobile, Alabama. In 1907 back on this side of the Atlantic, he stood as a Conservative in Battersea in 1907 and again for London County Council the following year. In 1910 he stood in Plymouth and was elected alongside Waldorf Astor. During the Great War he was a member of David Lloyd George's Ammunitions Committee. In 1918 he stood for the Plymouth Drake constituency and was again successful. Knighted that same year, he was to hold his Plymouth seat until 1929 during which time he was created a baronet of Plymouth and sat as the director for the International Chamber of Commerce.

Having lost his seat here he went north and at the next election was returned as MP for Sheffield Park, a seat he held until 1935. The following year, aged 77, he was created Baron Glenravel of Kensington and entered the House of Lords, again alongside Lord Astor, sadly however he died soon afterwards, in June 1937.

Greeting from Sir ARTHUR SHIRLEY BENN, M.P.
(DRAKE DIVISION, PLYMOUTH.)

Arthur Shirley Benn, (left inset) and second from the left above, with a group of supporters including a lady with a very unusual hat (possibly his American wife Alys). Note that the lads on the BSA have neither hats nor helmets.

Margaret Mitchell in Gordon's MG F-type Magna in August 1941.

GORDON MITCHELL'S MG

DR 9629 was one of over 2000 vehicles (at that time a record locally) registered in Plymouth in 1932 and most of them, over 1600, were prefixed with the new JY lettering.

Neill says that his father, Gordon, who was then living with his parents at Rockville House and Park (now Dean Cross Fields), at the top of Pomphlett Hill, was very friendly with Richard Barton and the Barton family who owned the Morris showrooms on Mutley Plain and that he most likely bought the car from there. Although, he adds, it may have been a private sale. Given that W A Gordon Mitchell was only 17 in 1932, one suspects that he would not have been the first owner.

The car itself is an MG F-type Magna, and Neill says that only 1200 were ever built. The MG name was relatively new in 1932: the marque had been developed by Cecil Kimber a decade earlier. Kimber had been in charge of William Morris's Morris Garages (hence MG) which was the Morris agent in Oxford. In 1924 he started selling the basic new 1.8-litre Morris Oxford and modified it into an MG Super Sports. The new machines had a lightly tuned engine and a new look aluminium body.

With Morris having already built up one of the best reputations for reliability and service in the country the new marque was a great success. As each new Morris rolled off the production line, so Kimber proved astute at adapting the engines and dressing up the bodywork to fit into the new-look MG style.

Quieter, more stylish and cheaper than the French sports cars that had regularly been imported before that, MG entered the racing arena in 1930 and that same year Kimber got his hands on that year's Wolseley Hornet (essentially a slightly longer version of the Morris Minor) and turned it into the F-type MG Magna. With a 1271cc engine, the new car came in touring and sporting versions with another variant, a supercharged racing K3 Magnette, which won its class in the 1933 Mille Miglia race and won outright that year's Ulster Tourist Trophy race. Tweaked over the next few years, the MG became a real star on the British and European racing circuit.

The photo here was taken in 1941 and, says Neill, reflects 'what father used to say were the two loves of his life at the time, the MG and mother ... although he was not sure which was the highest priority.'

Gordon and Margaret had met when both were serving the Admiralty in Bath, and they had married in December 1940, thereby ending the former's bachelorhood. Neill adds that the MG was 'the pride and joy of his bachelor days, whilst articled at Body & Son Chartered Surveyors, 22 Lockyer Street.

'I do know that when with Body & Son (1934-38), father's main client was Great Western Estates, the GWR's property arm, and the task he enjoyed most was being Clerk of the Works laying out Looe Golf Course. The MG features more prominently in photos of the works than the works themselves!

An unusual view from inside the car. Most cars were really basic internally, although the picnic holder for the tea cup is an interesting extra!

MILLBRIDGE TOLL GATE

In 1525 the Wise family gave up the rights to the northern bank of Stonehouse Creek so that Sir Piers Edgcumbe, the then new owner of (East) Stonehouse, could construct Mill Bridge and 'certain corn mill upon the said work.'

In 1807 the Edgcumbes decided, 'for the first time in the memory of Man,' to impose tolls on the bridge and a gate was duly erected. This caused a huge public outcry and the mayor and corporation with a large crowd marched to the site to claim public right of way. On arriving they dismantled the gate and threw it in the creek. Whereupon 'the owner of the mill waxed wroth and made use of improper language to the mayor who fined him on the spot.'

In the subsequent court wrangle it was established that whilst the owners had been lax in enforcing their right, they were entitled to do so, so a compromise was reached whereby pedestrians went free and horses and vehicles were chargeable.

The potential income from this prompted major repairs to the bridge and led to a much improved road between 'Plymouth, New Passage and Stoke.'

In the event it wasn't until 1924, when there was a long-awaited review of local tolls, that the bridge was made free.

No cars to be seen in this turn of the century view of Millbridge and the toll gate, there seen to the left of the mill itself.

The car here is a 1923 Standard S4 Tourer and the photo would have been taken sometime before April 1924. The Bass sign is on the wall of the Edgcumbe Hotel then run by Benjamin Leatherby.

Three undated views of the toll gate at Pennycomequick at the bottom of Alma Road. At some point (see far right) the building served as a local Post Office.

PENNYCOMEQUICK

In the wake of the 1762 Turnpike Act a great number of roads were improved all around the country. The area around Plymouth was no exception. Being an especially undulating and hilly county, the roads of Devon left much to be desired generally as they did in the more immediate area.

Foremost among them was the route from 'the corner of the meadow at the east end of the bridge by the Lower Grist mills within the Borough of Plymouth' (located at what is the eastern end of Cobourg Street) to Saltash Passage and the ferry crossing into Cornwall.

At that time Saltash Passage was nominally, at least, a part of Cornwall and in the course of improving this road the Turnpike Trust (administered by Sir John St Aubyn, Sir John Glanville, Sir William Molesworth, Sir John Rogers, Sir Harry Trelawney and Sir Christopher Treife) erected a bridge at Weston Mill. This obviated the crossing of the ford there and thence, via Milehouse Hill along what would become Alma Road to Pennycomequick.

The Act was initially put in place to last 21 years but it was renewed several times (1777, 1802 and 1823). Following the passing of the Saltash Floating Bridge Act of 1832 there were yet more improvements made in the road from Saltash Passage to Plymouth and among the sites identified for a toll gate was Pennycomequick. The new road was opened in the summer of 1836.

In 1853 we find the toll house here being let for £200 per annum, and although this gate appears to have been freed sometime before those at Millbridge, Stonehouse and elsewhere, in 1924 – the building was operated for sometime as a Post Office – it wasn't until around that time that the building was removed in order to improve the traffic flow around this busy junction.

Top: Pennycomequick with the old toll house visible to the right of centre at the bottom of Alma Road. Bottom: Same view, January 1925, the toll house has gone amid many other changes.

The drivers of two two solid wheeled vehicles paying their dues to cross Stonehouse Bridge, while a cyclist looks on, waiting his turn. Right: A selection of tickets for what pedestrians called 'Ha'penny Bridge'.

STONEHOUSE BRIDGE

Of all the remaining toll houses around at the dawn of the 1920s none aroused greater ire than those controlling the flow of traffic, pedestrian and otherwise, over Stonehouse Bridge.

It had been back on Tuesday 4 August 1914 that a Select Committee of the House of Lords heard further evidence in the case for the Amalgamation of the Three Towns of Plymouth, Stonehouse and Devonport.

The first witness called for the day was, Dr William Corbett, Chairman of the Urban District Council of East Stonehouse. Dr Corbett made it quite clear that East Stonehouse supported the bill as long as it involved all Three Towns and not just two of them, he was also at pains to point out that the existence of tolls was a vexed question. He felt that the tolls would have been abolished years ago 'but for the fact that there were three authorities that could not agree.'

At that point Lord Bray asked him: 'Over which bridge do most foot passengers pass?'

To which Corbett replied: 'The lower Stonehouse Bridge.'

Lord Bray: 'And the majority of the people who pass from one town to the other each day have to pay the toll?'

'Yes.'

'How much is the toll?'

'It is a half-penny, and that passes you to and fro. If you pass over several times a day that amounts to a good sum.'

Indeed the cost of the paper reporting the story was just a penny, so imagine now the cost of the toll being half the cost of *The Herald* – just for foot passengers.

Questioned further by counsel, the witness stated that the amalgamation of Stonehouse with Plymouth alone would be merely tinkering with the matter, and while Stonehouse would lose her identity, she would be a much smaller factor in any negotiations and lose the support of the county.

Then, when asked by the Earl of Chichester if Stonehouse would still be dependent on Devonport, Dr Corbett said; 'Yes, we would have Devonport's electricity works in our centre, and we would be part of the Parliamentary Borough of Devonport.'

He then added that had there been no separate local government areas in the Three Towns the present state of affairs would not have existed for a fortnight.

After an adjournment for lunch the Plymouth case was concluded and at 7pm that evening Great Britain declared war on Germany. The following day, Devonport was scheduled to present its case opposing the Amalgamation Bill, however it was to no avail and Royal Assent for the bill was granted on Monday 10 August 1914. In the event it was to be another ten years before Dr Corbett's wish to see the tolls abolished became a reality.

Ha'penny Bridge at low tide.

LAIRA BRIDGE GATES

This toll house, like the ones at Stonehouse was actually on the bridge.

The Laira Bridge toll gate that was on the Modbury Road approaching the bridge.

While the last toll gates around the Three Towns were freed in 1924 there had been a number of others over the years at various locations – including those on the Saltash Road, Exeter Road, Tavistock Road (at the top of Alexandra Road) and on the Modbury Road – one at Cattedown Corner and the other here on Laira Bridge.

Run by the Laira Bridge Company, this toll house was closed in 1900 after it was purchased by Plymouth Corporation. Richard Nicholas was the last collector of tolls here, but there was still the other nearby toll house at the end of Laira Bridge which was run at that time by the Embankment Company. It is strange to think that for many years people had to pay at both if their direction of travel required it!

The bridge housing the Laira Bridge Gate had been opened on 14 July 1827 'on which day her Royal Highness the Duchess of Clarence (afterwards Queen Adelaide), and suite, first passed over it on her way to Plymouth.'

An early iron bridge, it was the brain child of James Meadows Rendel, who had previously worked with the great pioneer in that field, Thomas Telford. The new crossing replaced Lord Morley's 'flying bridge' at this location. Impelled across the water by an iron chain and capable of carrying wagons, carts, carriages and other vehicles with their horses attached, this service had greatly improved Plymouth's links with Wembury, Brixton, Yealmpton and the South Hams. The new bridge quite literally took this line of communication to the next level.

A Thorneycroft lorry, registered in Greater London, leaving Plymouth via Laira Bridge c1923.

EMBANKMENT GATE

Under the auspices of the Plymouth Embankment Company, John Parker (Lord Boringdon, later Earl of Morley), promoted, through Acts of Parliament, dated 1802 and 1803, the embankment of the western side of the Laira and the formation of the New Eastern Road which, at long last, bypassed the steep old route over Lipson Hill.

'Sirs for the road on the Laira's banks
Accept the weary horse's thanks.'

That was one of the couplets coined for the procession at the opening of the new flat route. It was the second major favour that Lord Boringdon had been responsible for and for which pedestrians and horses were mighty grateful: the other being the fine, embanked carriage drive of 1794, the Longbridge at Marsh Mills.

The payback for the wealthy landowners who effected such improvements to people's ability to move around from town to town was, of course, the tolls they could charge.

At various times there were the two toll houses on the Laira Bridge (see previous page) and one at Cattedown Corner. On the Exeter (London) Road at Crabtree, Fanning's Toll at Arnold's Point, at the west end of the Embankment (pictured below). On the Tavistock Road – at the top of Alexandra Road.

Curiously enough, no sooner had the last of all these tolls, both here and in other parts of the Three Towns, been freed than there was a flurry of activity as roads in the area were generally widened and improved. Much of this work was long overdue, largely thanks to the impact here and across the country of the petrol-driven motor car.

A 1924 Bayliss Thomas car heads into Plymouth via the Embankment Gate (West End).

Another local vehicle, registered in 1918, pays its due on the Embankment.

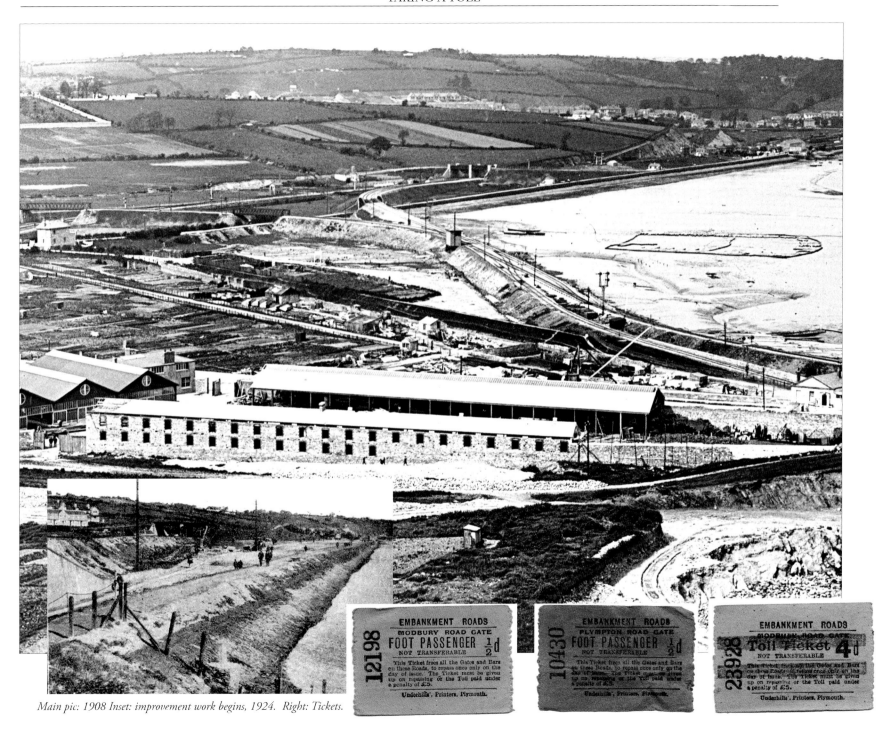

Main pic: 1908 Inset: improvement work begins, 1924. Right: Tickets.

EMBANKMENT ROADS
MODBURY ROAD GATE
12198 FOOT PASSENGER ½d
NOT TRANSFERABLE
This Ticket frees all the Gates and Bars
on these Roads, to repass once only on the
day of issue. The Ticket must be given
up on repassing or the Toll paid under
a penalty of £5.
Underhills', Printers, Plymouth.

EMBANKMENT ROADS
PLYMPTON ROAD GATE
10430 FOOT PASSENGER ½d
NOT TRANSFERABLE
This Ticket frees all the Gates and Bars
on these Roads, to repass once only on the
day of issue. This Ticket must be given
up on repassing or the Toll paid under
a penalty of £5.
Underhills', Printers, Plymouth.

EMBANKMENT ROADS
MODBURY ROAD GATE
23928 Toll Ticket 4d
NOT TRANSFERABLE
This Ticket frees all the Gates and Bars
on these Roads, to repass once only on the
day of issue. This Ticket must be given
up on repassing or the Toll paid under
a penalty of £5.
Underhills', Printers, Plymouth.

FREE ROADS

Stonehouse Bridge, was the last of three bridges and two additional toll gates to be declared free on 1 April 1924. All five locations were visited and officially freed on that day with a civic procession trailing around the various venues one after the other. A convoy of around 100 cars – a relatively unusual sight in 1924 – set out from Plymouth Guildhall at 11.45am led by the Mayor, Solomon Stephens, with his Deputy, Sir Thomas Baker, the Town Clerk, R J Fittall and a dignified collection of aldermen and councillors. At 11.53am they arrived at Laira Bridge where the civic party stepped out of their automobiles and Solomon Stephens solemnly snipped a ceremonial tape and declared 'this road free to the public of Plymouth forever.'

It was a phrase he was to repeat at each of the other ports of call.

But before setting off to toll gate number two Stephens was presented with a silver frame in which were mounted the last tickets to be issued at each of the gates.

The next of which, incidentally, was the neighbouring southern gate (Modbury Road) on the Embankment, on the edge of the Laira. The time of arrival there was 12.07pm and even allowing for another ceremony they were able to continue and reach their third point of call, the northern gate (Plympton Road) on the Embankment by 12.20pm.

With comparatively little other traffic on the roads they managed to motor along Old Laira Road, up Alexandra Road, along Braidwood Terrace (part of North Hill), then North Road, dropping down Eldad Hill to Millbridge, where they clocked in at 12.45pm.

So that the younger generation would come to appreciate the significance of these events hundreds of school children were congregated at Embankment Road, Millbridge and Stonehouse Bridge respectively where the civic party pulled up at 1pm.

Along the route the bells of Stoke Damerel and Saint George (Stonehouse) rang loud and clear and as they arrived back at the Guildhall for a grand luncheon, the bells of St Andrew chimed in honour of what was deemed to be a great event in the history of the relatively newly unified township of Plymouth. A loving cup was presented to the 60-year-old Mayor, who, curiously enough, was born in Embankment Road in 1864.

The son of a master baker, he would later enter the profession himself. Some years later he also entered politics and was successfully elected as Liberal in 1902. Twenty years later he was chosen to be Mayor and, somewhat unusually, was to hold the post for two years.

Over a decade later he was accorded the honour of becoming Lord Mayor of Plymouth and in that capacity greeted Her Majesty Queen Mary when she came to the city.

Images from 1 April 1924. Top and middle: Stonehouse Bridge.
Bottom: Freeing the Laira Bridge Toll Gate,
Mr Solomon Stephens (Mayor) cutting the tape.

At 12.07pm on 1 April 1924 the Mayor of Plymouth, Solomon Stephens, the Deputy Mayor, Sir Thomas Baker and the Town Clerk, Robert Fittall, passed through this gate and were followed by a cavalcade of around 100 cars. The vehicles were the first, officially, to pass without paying a toll.

SALTASH FERRY

The ferries deployed at Saltash were somewhat more modern than their counterparts at Torpoint, the one dating from 1892, the other from 1911, and both had single central platforms and so were better able to accommodate the automobile.

Nevertheless rising numbers of motor vehicles increased the urgency for bigger and better bridges, the first of which entered service in 1927.

Like the new, 1925, Torpoint Ferry, this was built by Philip & Son of Dartmouth, cost £8,950 and replaced the older of the two existing vessels.

A few years later Saltash Corporation had the opportunity to take advantage of a government job creation scheme and obtained a grant that enabled them to replace the 1911 floating bridge. Delivered at a cost of £10,750 it made its first crossings in 1933.

Royal Albert Bridge and Steam Ferry Boats, c1924.

The new ferry was 72ft long and 42ft wide, which made her 8ft longer and 6ft wider than her 1927 counterpart, and thus able to carry an extra row of vehicles and an extra vehicle in each row, giving her an increased capacity of around nine vehicles. Clearly this was an advantage that was acutely felt when bridge No2 was being rested and so it was that in 1938 Philip & Son were commissioned to cut No1 in half, lengthways, and insert a new section, and, at the same time to increase the length of the carriageway by 6ft. The livery of the new ferries incidentally was dark brown 'hull', buff upper body with a black funnel. The service operated between 6am and 11.15pm, although later bookings were available at a premium. Saltash cyclists and pedestrians crossed for free.

Top: One of the new floating bridges at Saltash. Above: A c1916 Model T Ford under Saltash Bridge, with Commanders Jimmy James and Williams seated in the back.

6 August 1928, Summer Bank Holiday congestion on the Torpoint Ferry, the 'queue of cars extends to the heart of Torpoint, besides the numerous cyclists awaiting passage."

Easter 1939 and 'the Torpoint Ferry had to cope with exceptionally heavy traffic throughout the day'.

TORPOINT FERRY

It wasn't until the 1920s that ferries designed to accommodate the motor car were put into service at Torpoint.

Until then this floating bridge service had taken pedestrians and horse-drawn traffic on two ferries that had been in service the in 1870s. The vessels were old and in desperate need of replacement, but Torpoint Urban Council was not in a position to commission new ferries and so the Ferries (Acquisition by Local Authorities) Act of 1919 came as a welcome move. The Act allowed Local Authorities, in this instance Cornwall County Council, to acquire the ferries and transfer them into Local Authority ownership.

The purchase was effected in 1922 at a cost of £42,000 and the passenger steamer Volta was instantly condemned and sold to be broken up at Cremyll. Meanwhile two new ferries were ordered, the first of which arrived in 1925. Built by Philip & Son of Dartmouth, the new bridge had a single, central traffic deck and had capacity for 800 passengers but only around 16 vehicles. The following year a second, Philips-built vessel entered the service and the other 1870s ferry was scrapped.

Pressure to improve the service yet further was increasing all the time however, and at the end of the 1920s Cornwall County Council succeeded in obtaining a bill to extend and enhance the crossing.

With powers to purchase land on both sides of the Tamar they set about demolition work, victims including the Ferry Hotel and part of Ferry Street on the Torpoint side and Royal Naval Engineering College boathouse on the Devonport side.

Work began in June 1930 and was completed two years later when a third ferry was brought into operation which now allowed for a two ferry service, capable of conveying thousands of passengers and over 60 vehicles per hour in each direction.

With waiting rooms on both sides of the river, new turnstiles and new offices at Torpoint and late night running in place, the new service was inaugurated on 1 July 1932.

Left and above: Work under way on improving the Torpoint Ferry operation.

The modernised Torpoint Ferry c1939.

PRATT'S SPIRIT
SIGN OF THE TIMES

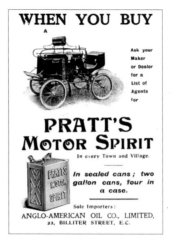

Oddly enough although this book is called *Plymouth in the Age of the Petrol-driven Motor Car* a title prompted by the imminent change to electric powered machines, prior to the 1930s most cars were powered by 'motor spirit'. Essentially this was indeed pretty much petrol as we know it but petrol (from the Latin petroleum – rock oil – from petra 'rock' and oleum 'oil') that term was a specific brand name, a name that initially described a solvent, a refined mineral oil product marketed by Carless, Capel & Leonard.

Founded in 1859 in Hackney Wick, East London, by the then aptly named Eugene Carless, the company went through various iterations during which Carless became the main distillery in Britain for newly imported American crude oil. With the invention of the combustion engine Frederick Simms, an associate of Gottlieb Daimler, suggested Petrol as a registered trade name but for the CC&L product and although William Leonard was happy with the idea, the Registrar's view was that the term was descriptive and therefore wasn't a valid contender for such a status. Furthermore it had already been in use for a number of years.

Carless, Capel & Leonard supplied their fuel for the celebrated London to Brighton Emancipation Run of 1896.

Meanwhile John Cassell a British publisher, coffee merchant and social campaigner, patented another product in 1862, named somewhat immodestly after himself – 'Cazeline Oil'. Described as being 'safe, economical and brilliant,' this oil it was claimed, 'possessed all the requisites which have so long been desired as a means of powerful artificial light.'

It wasn't long before someone in Ireland – Samuel Boyd in Dublin – started selling counterfeit cazeline. Cassell wrote to him requesting that he stop, but Boyd just changed the name for his counterfeit product to Gazeline which duly became gasoline when it was introduced to North America.

This page: Pratt's ads
Top l-r: 1902; 1904; 1909.

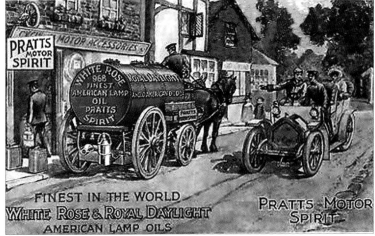

So it came to pass that the general descriptor for the fuel that powered most motor cars in this country was 'motor spirit.' It was a term that endured until the 1930s when Carless failed in another attempt to trademark the term 'petrol' which by then had become popular with the general public, so popular in fact that many of Carless's competitors started to adopt it.

Nevertheless the term 'motor spirit' had by then been utilized in various rules and regulations and so stuck in many quarters and in many documents.

Foremost among Britain's early motor spirit dealers was the Anglo-American Oil Company who, in that watershed year of 1896, started Pratt's Motor Spirit (although one early ad promoted Pratt's Petroleum).

Named in honour of the late Charles Pratt who, in his late 30s, had set up Charles Pratt & Co with Henry Rogers in 1867 and then subsequently joined forces with John D Rockefeller, who, aged 31, founded the Standard Oil Company, in 1870 and would go on to become one of the richest people the world had ever seen.

However it would be Pratt's name that was to be associated with the product that would come to underpin the dawn of the motor industry and that would pioneer many innovations in the trade.

Nowhere was this more apparent than in an article that appeared in the *Western Morning News* on Tuesday 16 July 1929. Under the heading 'ETHYL' IN DEVON the paper's Motoring Correspondent wrote the following: Ever in the forefront in matters associated with fuel for the internal combustion engine, Messrs Pratts have recently taken yet another highly important step in the service of motorists in offering them the remarkable new motor fuel known as Ethyl.

In the earliest days of the 'horseless carriage' Pratts was the first company to distribute throughout the entire country, and to introduce the familiar two gallon petrol can by arrangement with the Board of Trade.

As the motoring movement grew with amazing rapidity Pratts foresaw the need of speedier distribution methods and were the first petrol distributing company to introduce petrol pumps. They were also the first with the sealed and guaranteed pumps now universally adopted. Again with the unceasing tendency towards high compression engines, Pratts met the situation with Pratts' Ethyl petrol now world renowned for its remarkable anti knock properties.

Top: With no hint of irony, Pratt's motor spirit delivered by horse. Right: Pratt's typical two gallon can.

'I yesterday had an opportunity of testing thoroughly the new spirit over the hills and dales of Devon.

NO "PINKING"

'A four-years-old car of about 20 horsepower rating of a well-known make was selected for the run, a car which, so I was informed, had done about 30,000 miles and with ordinary petrol was particularly addicted to knocking and pinking. The day was particularly hot, and from the first a steady run at forty miles an hour, with hills taken in our stride produced no suggest of over-heating.

An ad for the original two-gallon can and two ads for the pioneering 'Golden Pump' - the first to break through the two-can approach. Top: Ads targeting the lady driver.

'There were demonstrations of quick and easy acceleration through Plympton's traffic-congested streets and the worth of the spirit in Devon's tortuous roads, where quick and easy overtaking in such stretches of straight road that occur is essential, was apparent in the first four miles of the run.

'It might be said here that from the first to last, through some of the stiffest hills in the country were negotiated with maximum gradients as great as 1 in 4 or 1 in 31/2 there was never a knock or a sign of pinking.

'At Ivybridge we were brought to a full stop on the bridge a the foot of the hill leading out of the village, by traffic, but at the stiffest part of the hill a comfortable thirty miles an hour was being registered by the speedometer. There was heavy tar on this road, but third gear took us up without a sign of strain on the part of the engine, and not a suspicion of a knock.

'The most drastic tests were those of Peek Hill which is about 2000 yards long and has a maximum gradient of 1 in 5.

'Under the railway bridge we brought the car to a standstill and commencing the climb the car was brought from fourth to third gear in three lengths and so to second and a good speed was maintained, despite the attention of Dartmoor ponies wandering across the road.

'Why, one asks, does Ethyl petrol eliminate the knock? It is because the fluid controls the combustion rate of petrol. It keeps it from burning too quickly in the presence of carbon, and at high termperature and each explosion produces a powerful, even push, instead of a series of hammerlike blows.

A PENNY WELL SPENT

'Ethyl costs a penny per gallon more than standard spirit, but one has little hesitation in saving both to tourists for whom Devon hills have certain terrors, and for residents in the county, who would make their motoring more enjoyable by reason of that additional power – and mileage – which it gives, it is a penny remarkably well spent.

'Devon, incidentally, has been selected from the whole of the areas in England for the launching of a campaign to bring this new spirit more fully before the motorists of this country, and this week in the county is 'Ethyl Week'.

'That fact that it was Ethyl spirit that brought the Schneider trophy to England in 1927 was revealed at a lunch held in Plymouth to inaugurate this week's experiment in Devon.

'Mr G Bass said Ethyl was not the product of mere accident but the result of many scientific tests and steady endeavour, some 30,000 experiments having been conducted before tetra-ethy lead was discovered. Ethyl was introduced into England at the beginning of last year, in the knowledge that there were such developments in the motor industry which made such a fuel inevitable and a necessity.

'It was the knowledge that the numbers of cars were going to Devon and the West for summer tours which led Messrs Pratts to select the area as the basis for an intensified campaign to consolidate the effects of previous good work in the bringing Ethyl to the notice of motorists.

'Mr PGA Smith said Devon was selected because it was difficult to indicate an area in England where local newspapers had greater power and prestige.'

The lead in the petrol would, in time, become problematic, as indeed would Pratts' desire to advertise their products in hitherto unprecedented ways. Nevertheless the product remained one of Britain's best loved brands, although in 1935 Anglo-American Oil replaced the name Pratt with Esso, this being the phonetic pronunciation of the original initials of the company Standard Oil – S.O.

9 January 1924: Dismantling and removing near Plymouth (bottom of Colesdown Hill, Billacombe) a Pratt's Perfection roadside sign following the decision of Anglo-American Oil Co. to discard such advertisements, and thus assist in preserving the natural beauties of the landscape. Left: A restored Pratt Albion lorry.

DELAFEILDS

Telegrams "Delafeild, Cycles, Plymouth."   Telephone 0940.

Plymouth Motor Garage
and Cycle Depot. . . .

HUMBER CYCLES & MOTORS
—HUMBER CARS.

"In all the World Unequalled."

Call and see our Special Humber Free Wheel, Two
Brakes, every thing reliable,

£8 8s 0d.

R. B. DELAFEILD

33, Frankfort Street,
PLYMOUTH.

Cars Stored by the Day, Week, Month or Year.
Inspection Pits.

REPAIRS BY MOTOR EXPERTS.
—— PETROL. OIL. GREASE.

Any make Car supplied at market prices, and
driven to destination by expert drivers.

Above: 1903 advertisement for Delafeild in Frankfort Street. Right: Undated promotional ashtray for Delafeilds, note the early telephone number – Plymouth 318.

William Delafeild appears to have had ten children, which was not unusual for someone born near the beginning of the nineteenth century. Two of the boys would share the same middle name, Richard Bawden Delafeild and Charles Bawden Delafeild. Richard would also go on to have ten children, nine of them girls and his only son was destined to share his father's initials – Reginald Baker Delafeild. Brother Charlie meanwhile sired just eight children, four of whom were destined to die young and one of whom Alfred, was to inherit the Bawden middle name.

Clearly then the Delafeild family was a large one and seemingly a prosperous one too, as Charles ran a successful boot making business, while Richard was one of the first cycle dealers in town and son Reginald would become one of the first motor dealers in the area. At one point all three were operating their businesses and, it would appear, all living in Frankfort Street (roughly where the western end of New George Street now sits), at numbers 21, 32 and 33.

Richard was a particularly prominent proponent of cycling, and in the summer of 1897 was the principal steward for the first championship meeting held in the Devon and Cornwall Centre of the National Cyclists Union. It took place on Saturday 19 June and 'drew to it some of the finest amateur and professional riders of the day.'

However the press report noted that 'Circumstances were against a big financial success. In the morning the sky was very threatening, but no rain until before commencement of the meeting. A start once made, it continued to rain all the afternoon, the downfall becoming heavier as time proceeded. The final race for the afternoon, the 25 Mile Amateur Championship, was ridden with rain pouring pitilessly.' Nevertheless around 3,000 people attended the event.

Some years earlier, incidentally, Richard had been race secretary for the Three Towns Wheelers' event staged at Home Park in conjunction with the Devonport Cycling Club and before that even, in 1892, he'd been a subscriber looking to establish a racecourse for Plymouth – one that could be utilised for 'football, cricket, athletic and cyclist gatherings.'

Unfortunately Richard died, aged 60, in 1909 but the business continued and for a while remained in Frankfort Street. Meanwhile Reginald moved eastwards to Bedford Street (which then fed into Frankfort Street), where they now operated as Delafeilds Motor and Cycle Dealers. They not only sold cars and cycles but rented them out as well – three pounds a day for a car in 1909.

At some point Reginald's nephew, Alfred Bawden Delafield joined the business, but tragically he was to die, aged 45, following a car crash on Easter Saturday, April 1939.

Alfred had driven an open top MG to Weymouth to meet Lieutenant Bennington of Portland who was interested in buying the car. On the way back from Dorset he encountered a car driven by a Miss P Cornick who was not the owner of the vehicle. There were two other Bridport residents in the car at the time, Miss F Cornick and Mr Reginald Good, whose vehicle it was. Striking the other vehicle, which had evidently strayed some way out onto the crown of the road, the unfortunate Mr Delafeild's MG flipped and landed upside down at right angles to the road with him trapped beneath it. Death was not instant but came in hospital the following day. The subsequent inquest decided there was insufficient evidence to apportion any blame for the accident. The funeral, held at St Augustine's in Alexandra Road (where the Delafeild enterprise was then based) was attended by a great many family, friends, freemasons and business associates, including his business partner RR Rodd, secretary Miss Beer, a number of Delafeild's staff – W Griffin, E Mark, A Tucker, D Rendle, H Abbott, and R Hollett – and representatives of almost every garage and car showroom business in the area.

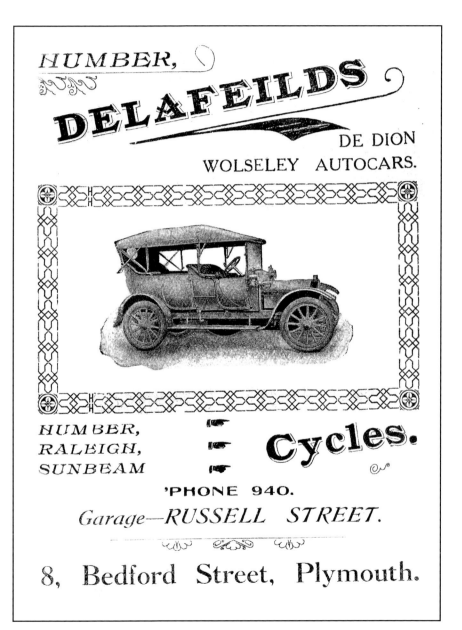

HUMBER,

DELAFEILDS

DE DION
WOLSELEY AUTOCARS.

HUMBER,
RALEIGH,
SUNBEAM ☞ Cycles.

'PHONE 940.

Garage—RUSSELL STREET.

8, Bedford Street, Plymouth.

THE CO-OP CONSIDERS

Within the Co-operative society locally and within society as a whole, there was still a place for the horse. Ten years on from Royle's report on Road Transport for the Co-operative Societies, the traffic manager of Leeds Industrial Co-operative Society, J S Holloway, prepared a similar report, this time for the Eleventh Co-operative Trades and Business Conferences, 1931.

'There is no doubt,' he wrote, 'the petrol machine holds the premier position in mechanical transport, and so far as the heavier types are concerned there are many points in its favour.'

However Holloway was clearly a champion of the horse: 'There is no doubt that under certain conditions the horse can compete successfully with the motor, and I now propose to indicate how it can be determined as to when those conditions are favourable to the employment of horse vehicles.'

He then went to great lengths, employing a variety of statistical formula and equations, to argue that horse transport held an advantage 'where the distance to be travelled is a comparatively short one, where the streets are narrow and congested, or where the condition of the road is bad'.

Holloway further recognised that the electric vehicle too, now had a place: 'Under favourable conditions, (it) has certain advantages over the petrol motor, in relation to cleanliness and simplicity of construction, but the factors which mitigate against its use for ordinary work are: Its restricted mileage, the heavy cost of batteries both for replacement and maintenance, its very moderate speed, especially in hilly districts, and, above all, the lack of facilities for battery charging at mid-day and during the night.'

The good news in relation to motor vehicles appeared to be their improved reliability. In Holloway's own garage, he was employing one mechanic for every ten vehicles ... 'and as we do all our own maintenance work, I think this may be taken as a fair indication of any society's requirements so far as staff is concerned when mechanics are employed.'

As for the life expectancy of the vehicles: 'In our case all rolling stock is depreciated according to rule at the rate of 15% per annum, and this practically compels us to fix the life of a motor at not less than seven years. We find that in relation to the lighter type it is advisable to dispose at the end of the seventh year, but that heavier lorries can reasonably be carried for a longer period.'

Year.	H.P. Class.	Motor Cycles.	Goods Vehicles.	Motor Hackneys.	All Mechanically Propelled Vehicles (Excluding Tram-cars and Trade Licenses).
1922...	314,769	377,943	150,995	77,614	952,474
1923...	383,525	430,138	173,363	85,965	1,105,657
1924...	473,528	495,579	203,156	94,153	1,299,824
1925...	579,901	571,552	224,287	98,833	1,509,786
1926...	676,207	629,648	248,367	99,077	1,689,722
1927...	778,056	671,620	275,831	95,676	1,858,794
1928...	877,277	690,672	294,190	93,429	1,995,827
1929...	970,275	705,025	318,253	95,798	2,130,628
1930...	1,042,258	698,878	334,237	98,865	2,217,609

4. No one can predict with certainty for how long, and to what extent, the total will go on increasing. Some authorities think this country's motor traffic must be near saturation point. They might change their minds if they spent a few days in New York or other big American cities ; they may be influenced, too, by the following figures :—

Country.	Persons per Motor Vehicle.	Country	Persons per Motor Vehicle.
U.S.A.	4.9	Union of S. Africa (All)	62.4
New Zealand (White)	9.1	Great Britain	34
,, ,, (All)	9.6	France	37.4
Canada	9.1	Belgium	70.1
Australia	13.2	Germany	117.2
Union of S. Africa (White)	13.9	Italy	215.5

1936, Plymouth Co-operative Society Albion removal van.

Old Town Street c1909 with a single car, is it one of Walter's, parked outside his garage.

WALTER WILLIAMS
FIRST LOCAL PETROL STATION?

One of Plymouth's pioneers in the age of the petrol-driven motor car was Walter Williams. Born in Bridgenorth, Shropshire in 1876, the son of a draper, in his early twenties he was working as a cycle salesman in Portsmouth.

On 1 February 1904 he married 19-year-old local girl, Emily Farling in St Paul's Church, Southsea, and later that year we find him operating as motor engineer from their premises in the then newly built block between the similarly newly constructed Drake Circus and Park Street at 118 Tavistock Road.

The following year he opened a new facility just down the road in another modern development in Old Town Street. In February 1905 he took out an advertisement in the local press: Walter Williams' Motors – Wherever you see a MOTOR think of WALTER WILLIAMS. I hope you will associate WILLIAMS with MOTORS and MOTORS with WILLIAMS … that you always think of one with the other.'

In April that year he was promoting the latest Darracq motor cars. Alexandre Darracq had started out manufacturing bicycles and sold his first company for a pretty penny enabling him to start up a new venture, in 1898, making bicycle parts, tricycles and quadricycles, moving on to his first motorcycle, then a three-wheeled car before producing his first four-wheeled vehicle with an internal combustion engine, in 1900.

In 1902 he sold his new enterprise to an English outfit who adopted the name A Darracq and Company Limited. By 1903 they were offering four different wooden plated chassis models from a 1.1 litre single cylinder engine, through a 1.9 litre twin to a 3.4 litre four.

Converting to a steel chassis the following year, sales were growing quickly and the factory was expanded by over 50%, meanwhile Darracqs, by 1905, were able to claim that their cars held all six speed records then known in the world of motor cars.

Small wonder that Walter Williams was able to state with some confidence that same year that the 8, 12, 15 and 30 horse-power Darracqs that he was selling were 'grand hill climbers' built to 'special specification for Devonshire hills.'

He further made a point of saying 'Clients waited upon in Devon and Cornwall.'

In other words although he had a splendid showroom in town, he was happy to deliver cars around the two counties.

Later that summer another Williams advertisement, this time in the *Western Evening Herald*, boasted that he had 'Everything for Motorists in Stock … Continental, Clincher, Michelin, Shell, Pratt, Prices, Vacuum. Up-to-date Charging Plant always open. Wholesale or Retail.'

And in October he announced that he had 'several thoroughly reliable second-hand cars for sale' and was 'open to reasonable offers.'

These were very early days in the trade locally. Old Town Street was undoubtedly at the heart of one of the most modern shopping areas in the country at that time and Walter's business clearly went from strength to strength. His career was not without its setbacks however.

On Friday 1 May 1908 he was driving past the newly opened (1903) Salisbury Road School just after four o'clock when six-year-old Violet Chapman stepped into the road, in front of Walter's car. He was, by all accounts, travelling at a moderate pace and had three other gentlemen in the vehicle – Captain Daniels, Lieutenant Dalrymple RN, and Stanley Vosper, of Merafield, Plympton. Poor Violet was knocked down and apparently died instantly. Walter drove her to the South Devon and East Cornwall Hospital (Greenbank) but there was nothing that could be done. *The Herald* reported that 'the child's parents keep a grocer's shop in Exeter Street and are naturally greatly distressed.'

A massive understatement no doubt, but motoring was then still in its infancy, people of all ages weren't car-aware in the way that was later to become almost instinctive, and car accidents like that were not uncommon. Doubtless Walter too was greatly distressed as by that time he had two very young daughters of his own, Emily and Mary.

There was another accident, of a different kind, the following year, when several boys found Walter's open-sided car outside his garage and pushed it forwards causing it to roll into the plate glass window of Curtis's bookshop in Drake Circus. The glass was broken, but covered by insurance, the bookcase, however, and a couple of books were not covered and represented a loss of around ten shillings!

As well as being one of the local pioneers of the trade in motor cars, it would appear that Walter was at the forefront of developments locally when it came to petrol stations.

Prior to the end of the Great War there was no such thing as a petrol station, the first generation of motorists had to buy their fuel from chemists, hardware shops, roadside hotels ... and from garages. However there were no petrol pumps in any of these places, as petrol was generally supplied in two-gallon cans.

The first filling station as such in England, it would appear, was at Aldermaston, Berkshire and it opened in November 1919 – or

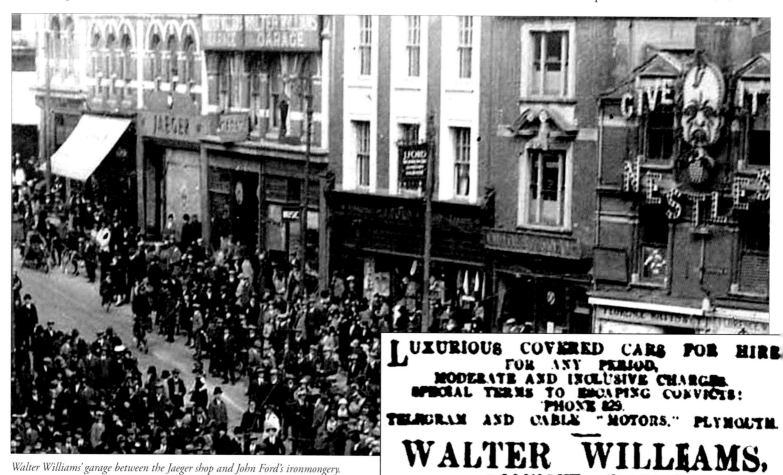

Walter Williams' garage between the Jaeger shop and John Ford's ironmongery.

March 1920 – there appears to be a degree of uncertainty, but either way it would make it 100 years ago, that such a facility first existed in this country.

It was operated by the AA (Automobile Association who had started out back in 1905) and uniformed men were employed to supply petrol – specifically National Benzole – British-made fuel to counter the trade in petrol coming in from Russia which, post the 1917 Bolshevik Revolution, seemingly gave the impression that the UK condoned the situation there.

With the motor trade enjoying something of a post-war boom, the petrol station idea, which had already been going for a dozen or so years in America, caught on rapidly: the AA created seven in quick succession, each solely for the exclusive use of AA members (and presumably definitely not RAC members – the RAC being the senior of the two organisations having formed back in 1897). The idea was an obvious one that was bound to prove popular and within three years there were some 7000 petrol stations in more general use across the country.

And, in Plymouth, it would appear that the very first was operated by Walter Williams whose wayside filling station was at Crabtree on the way out of Plymouth, doubtless to appeal to those headed out of town on a longer run than could be fuelled by a two gallon can (although most drivers carried their own back-up supply).

The site was near the erstwhile Rising Sun pub (later to be known as the Roundabout and demolished in the 1980s) at Marsh Mills. The business was by no means straightforward though.

On 3 November 1925 Walter had received a letter from the secretary of the Motor Trade Association stating that he was alleged to have infringed the price and if he wished he could appear before the committee in London ... the next day. There was apparently no real indication as to the nature of the charge and Walter requested an adjournment, however the Stop List Committee met in his absence, adjudicated on the case and fined Walter £12 (around £750 today).

It subsequently transpired that a lad employed by Walter at the Crabtree filling station had sold 'motor spirit to the Stop List Superintendent for 1/5d instead of 1/7d (i.e. around 6p instead of 7p, although in today's terms one shilling would be worth around £2.50). Walter insisted that his records showed that what had been sold was No.3 spirit which did actually retail for 1/5d so there was no offence.

The Motor Traders' Association had been formed back in 1910, essentially to protect the wholesale and retail prices of cars, but theu had gradually extended their remit.

In November 1926 Walter told a *Western Morning News* representative that he was not a member of the Motor Traders' Association, and had not signed the agreement form which had been sent out by the combine in the petrol 'war'.

'We encourage competition as regards the supply of petrol,' he said. 'It has been stated that petrol is worth what it will fetch. That is correct and we do not want to see the price soar to the level of 4/6d, which it did during the war. Judging from the report of the interview in the *Western Morning News* Mr Williams added, 'It looks as if the Russian Oil Products intend having their own filling stations. It would seem therefore that they do not anticipate the support of the trader very much.' Mr Williams added that he had in mind the question of installing extra pumps at his filling station at Crabtree, but he would not say whether or not at present he was considering adding pumps which would supply 'pirate' spirit.

YOUR PATRONAGE much appreciated at
Our Filling Station, near Rising Sun, Laira.
All Brands.

WALTER WILLIAMS,
118, Tavistock-road, PLYMOUTH.

Walter Williams advert from March 1926 (was this Plymouth's first filling station? It was on the long left hand bend after Crabtree and before the Rising Sun, on the then A38.

AC LEMPRIERE BACK
ABBEY GARAGE

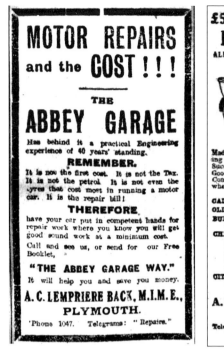

In 1897, the year he became an associate member of the Institute of Mechanics, 33-year-old Arthur Charles Lempriere Back arrived in Plymouth to work in the Devon and Cornwall Ice and Cold Storage Company in St Andrew Street. In the days before electric domestic refridgerators and indeed the widespread availability of electricity, the manufacture of ice and the ability to offer cold storage was by no means commonplace.

Arthur was a Norfolk boy and had been educated at Great Yarmouth Grammar School. Soon after leaving school he had spent a few years working on an orange plantation in America before coming back to Britain and serving an apprenticeship as an engineer in Dartford.

The fifth son and the ninth child (of 11) of Henry and Fanny Lempriere, Arthur was an ambitious young man. He became an early member of the South Devon Automobile Club and in 1907, still working with the ice works, he started a side line as a mechanical motoring engineer. In 1911, now living in Brandreth Road, with his wife Mary, whom he married ten years earlier, Arthur bought numbers 39 and 40 St Andrew Street, opposite the ice works and opened up a formal garage business. The following year he added numbers 2 and 4 Finewell Street to his fledgling empire thereby creating the opportunity to knock through into the adjacent street.

During the Great War the garage continued to operate, although in October 1914 a miniature rifle range was opened in the premises, it was for the use of the National Reserve and the Plymouth Citizens' Defence Force. Meanwhile Arthur served a period as a lieutenant in the 1st Volunteer Battalion of the Devon Regiment at Okehampton, acting as a workshop officer.

After the war he threw himself wholeheartedly into his enterprise, now known as Abbey Garage (on account of its proximity to the misnamed Abbey or Prysten House and the Abbey Hotel in St Andrew Street – now known as Kitty's).

Anxious to corner the market for repairs he astutely bagged the telegram address of 'Repairs, Plymouth'. His approach was underlined in one of the early ads for Abbey Garage, which very much sums up the state of motoring 100 years ago:

'REMEMBER.

'It is not the first cost. It is not the Tax. It is not the petrol. It is not even the tyres that cost the most in running a motor car. It is the repair bill!

THEREFORE, 'have your car put in the competent hands for repair work where you know you will get good sound work at a minimum cost. Call and see us, or send for our Free Booklet – *The Abbey Garage Way* – it will help you and save you money.

Abbey Garage wasn't only a repair station however, as Arthur sold cars, vans and lorries as well. Indeed he specialised in foreign vehicles and regularly advertised Cadillacs, Oldsmobiles, Buicks and Chevrolets. One 1920 Chevrolet he advertised as 'The Business Man's Car, with electric lighting and starting and right hand steering.' It was, he claimed very light on fuel and guaranteed to be able to do 40 mph. It wasn't cheap however, and was on sale for a cool £435, no small sum back then. It was cheaper than another marque that Abbey Garage sold, the Ruston Hornsby. This British beast was developed by Edward Boughton who had joined the Lincoln based Ruston Hornsby Company in 1916 after helping to develop the tank. His cars were quite heavy and came in two models, one with a 2614cc engine, the other with a 3308cc engine. The cheapest was around £440 while the top of the range model went out for nearly £1000. Unfortunately for all concerned neither model really took off and between 1919 and 1924 only 1,500 were made.

Even more unfortunately for ACLB, he never lived to see how that saga panned out as he passed away, in 1923, in Woodside Nursing Home, at the age of 59, after 'a few days illness.' A member of Emmanuel Church Parochial Council and a prominent local freemason, he and Mary had no children.

A relative, Major Charles Holthouse was drafted in to run the place but he appears to have had no long term interest in the business and in 1926 an offer for the sale of Abbey Garage and adjoining properties was made to the Corporation for their consideration for use as a Fire Brigade Station, but the offer wasn't taken up and so it came to pass that in December 1927 Messrs Mumford's Engineering Repair Works purchased the premises and moved their base to Abbey Garage.

Top: July 1915 potential recruits photographed on the tram lines at the bottom of Old Town Street with St Andrew's Church in the background and a sign for Abbey Garage just visible in St Andrew Street.

MUMFORDS

The son of a farmer from Shaugh Prior, Joseph Mumford was working as a teenage apprentice wheelwright in the Stonehouse part of Union Street in 1851. By 1860 it would appear that he had branched out on his own and become a full time wheelwright, with his two eldest sons John and Joseph subsequently joining him in the Mumford & Sons business that had been established on Mutley Plain.

By 1890 with both boys now well into their 20s, the enterprise had been restyled as coachbuilders and wheelwrights and was based in Grosvenor Lane, just off Mutley Plain. Joseph senior and his wife Emeline now had two more sons, William, aged 12, and Frank, aged 6, as well as four daughters (and another who died in infancy).

For some reason William, on turning 21, opted not to stay with his older brothers (Joseph senior had died, aged 58, in 1892), but to start his own, under his own name. Moving closer to the main business quarter of Plymouth he established his own enterprise in Glanville Street in 1900.

William Mumford

With one eye firmly fixed on the future William's new business was one of the first in the area to fully embrace the motor car as part of his carriage building concern.

It was a shrewd move and turnover for the first year was reported to be around £500, a figure that increased five-fold within four years to £2,500 (over £300,000 today).

Motor vehicles were still a rare sight on local roads, but William was undoubtedly aware of the direction of travel, indeed it is said that he built the first car body in the Westcountry – on a 40/45 hp Ariel-Simplex chassis.

In 1903, having outgrown Glanville Street, William Mumford, now just 25, moved his fledgling business into new premises in Ebrington Street. The street, incidentally, had only recently been widened to accommodate the electric tram, a service that took its feed from the newly opened power station at Prince Rock. The northern side of the street had been entirely rebuilt following the widening of the thoroughfare.

Around this time William Mumford claimed another first when he built the first motor taxi in Plymouth. Constructed on the chassis of a model T Ford, the finished product was sold to Jack Andrew of Andrew's Garage.

Meanwhile, back at Mutley Plain (No68), with additional workspace in Carlisle Avenue/Belgrave Lane, the Mumford & Son business had also added the motor car to its repertoire, while the oldest of the brothers, John, was operating a separate cycle business at No58.

Above: Mumford's Ebrington Street premises.
Below: 1911 Hurtu ad, Mumfords.

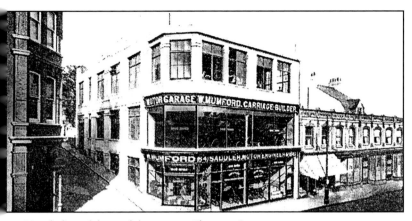

Mumford's workshop and showroom in Ebrington Street

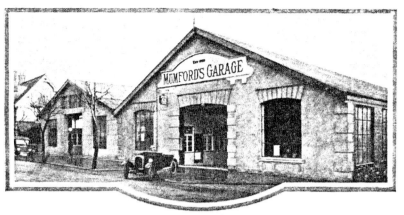

Head Offices and Garage, Salisbury Road, Plymouth.

William was unlikely to ever be eclipsed by the other side of the family however and in 1908 he started the first motor bus service between Plymouth and Crownhill, deploying a De Dion Bouton vehicle to run the route that ran along Mutley Plain.

That same year Orville and Wilbur Wright demonstrated yet another technological advance in transport when they took to the air in one of their flying machines at Le Mans, in France. It was their first European display and came just five years after their first successful ground defying efforts Stateside, in their pioneering power-driven, heavier-than-air machine.

Four years later, in 1912, William Mumford started to work on his own flying machine, but eventually abandoned the effort on account of not being able to find a satisfactory engine for the job. The corps business continued to grow meanwhile and it wasn't long before the Ebrington Street site had become inadequate and the company found themselves working 'under great difficulties'. In 1914 William acquired a sizeable site in Salisbury Road and the following year a garage measuring 173ft by 60ft (roughly 53x18 metres) was erected there. However 'in just over two years we were turning customers away for want of room.

'We then proceeded to cover the remainder of the property with buildings and at the present time we have three-quarters of an acre of floor space at Salisbury Road.' So ran the wording of a brochure celebrating the 25 years of W Mumford Ltd as the company was now registered. The narrative continued: 'When the final additions were commenced it was our intention to do all the work here – up to then the body building having been done at Ebrington Street and the engineering at Salisbury Road – but we soon realised that we should have been congested from the start. So we went further afield and purchased a site of five acres at Billacombe, just a mile outside the Plymouth boundary, which appeared to us to be the most suitable for our purpose.'

The site at Billacombe was purchased in 1920, William had transformed the operation into a limited company in August 1923 and the following year his sons Clarence (23) and William Roy (21) joined the firm with the former taking on the role of sales manager and the latter being put in charge of sales and publicity.

The anniversary brochure then took us inside the Salisbury Road site: 'Recognising that one of the chief features necessary in an up-to-date garage is ease of ingress and egress, W. Mumford built the garage and service station at Salisbury Road so that each one of the 200 cars that the buildings are capable of housing, could be moved without disturbing the remainder. These premises, which cover three-quarters of an acre of ground are of lofty construction, giving a maximum amount of light and air and have no less than five separate entrances. 'An efficient and willing staff aided by every modern convenience is always on hand to attend to your requirements. A curbside pump delivers petrol from a 2,000 gallon Bowser underground tank and air for tyre inflation is supplied from an electric pump. Light repairs, service adjustments, battery charging, etc, are carried out here while larger jobs are consigned to the Works at Billacombe.

'The personal comfort of the motorist has been well looked after, both ladies' and gentlemen's toilets being provided.

'The garage charges are extremely moderate especially in view of the first class service we offer. A limited number of private lock-up garages are available and ours is the only garage in the locality that can comfortably accommodate heavy lorries and trailers.

The washing and polishing of cars is competently carried out by a staff of cleaners who have due respect for paint, varnish – and the owners feelings; 'A photo of a section of the garage during our 'Annual Motor Show'. This is a little affair which we hold in the spring of each year, the exhibits consisting of cars, motor coaches, saloon buses, bodywork,polished chassis, accessories, etc, etc.'

Top: Mumford's 1923 display with a Durant for sale on the left for £195, and two BSA models to the right. Bottom: Mumford's BC 1923 touring car – a promotional gimmick for the 2nd Annual Western Motor Show, AD 1923.

Another motor show shot, with BSA, Bianchi, Austin and Hurtu models on display as well as, to the left of the Hurtu, a chassis to show the raw material that Mumfords worked with.

The Drake Circus showroom at night.

Left and above: The general showrooms at Drake Circus with a Riley sports in the foreground.

Next up was an account of the main showrooms in town: 'Old Town Street, our special Daimler and BSA showrooms. Here is to be found a comprehensive selection from the 50 different models of the Daimler and BSA range. It may be mentioned in passing that these are by far the largest and best appointed showrooms in the district being capable of housing well over a dozen cars. 'Little need be said about the Daimler – it being acknowledged as one of the world's best cars – except that smaller models than heretofore are now being marketed at prices well within the reach of persons of moderate income. Since its reintroduction in 1922, the popularity of the BSA light car has increased by leaps and bounds. 'The 10hp air-cooled model in particular having covered itself with glory (and trophies) in various reliability trials. We are special agents for Daimler and BSA cars for the West of England.'

'Over twenty years of experience with practically every make of car has enabled us to select and recommend with confidence the following cars (in addition to the Daimler and BSA) Willys-Knight, Riley, Swift, Overland and Durant Cars, and Leyland, Reo, SPA, G&J, Daimler and Republic commercial vehicles, representative models being always on view.

'In addition these premises are fully stocked with a large and varied range of accessories, gadgets and tyres – remember our slogan 'W Mumford, Ltd., everything for the motorish' [sic].

'By the way, the mechanically inclined may be interested in the way we get the cars up to the second floor, shown at the back of the photo. In order to do this we have installed a ramp 10ft by 15ft which is hinged at one end, the other being elevated by twin screws, operated by worm gearing – the whole being designed and manufactured at our Billacombe works. The ramp then forms an inclined plane between the first and second floors up which the cars are run under their own power.

Corner of the Machine Shop.

Universal Milling Machine.

Section of Stores.

Specimens of our Handicraft.

Another view of the Machine Shop.

Left: Page from brochure showing Machine Shop. Above: Mumfords Billacombe Works.

While the showrooms in town may have represented the public face of Mumfords, the business end of the operation was the Works at Billacombe. These were described at the time as being a one-and-a-half acre site situated 'one mile outside the Plymouth border on the main road to Kingsbridge.

The narrative continued: 'The natural lighting scheme of these premises is carried out in such a way that there are no dark corners. As a matter of fact, on a dull day it is lighter indoors than out. After dark the shops are brilliantly lit with high candle power electric lamps, the current being generated on the premises. 'The Engineering Shop measures 150ft by 60ft. Here are carried out repairs and overhauls of every description, our facilities being such that we can take on anything from decarbonising to a complete overhaul with equal ease. The shop is staffed with highly skilled mechanics who do their work well – and quickly. The machine shop is equipped with the best and most up-to-date plant, including universal milling machines, lathes, shapers, drilling machines, power hacksaws, universal grinders, crank shaft grinders, 300 ton power hydraulic press, etc. Power is supplied by a 85hp semi-Diesel engine.

'Our spacious stores are stocked with a wide range of spare parts, every size ball-bearing and popular size solid tyres.

'Body shops. You've possibly come across "Mumford" Bodies during your travels. They give complete satisfaction wherever they go, as witness repeat orders from places as remote as Guernsey, Isle of Man, Isle of Wight and Sunderland.

Young men at Mumfords learning the trade.

Above: Note how the basic chassis is slowly built up. Left: Completed vehicles including a Vulcan saloon.

Top: left Mill, right Panel beating section. Middle: left Sawing sheds, right, Framers Shop. Bottom: left, Painting and Finishing Shop, right, Timber shed.

The Works themselves comprised 'five single storey buildings: Woodworking shop, painting and finishing, dry timber shed, saw mill and smith shop. Here we have a full range of wood-working machinery, comprising circular saws, planing and thickening machines, band saws, tenoning machines

'List of bodies for which we can quote prices: Touring Cars, Landaulettes, Saloons, All-weathers, Saloon Buses, Motor Coaches, Lorries and Vans.

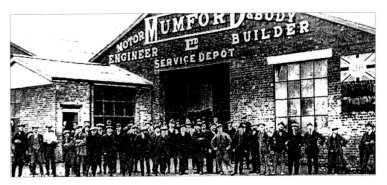

'Our designs are right up to date and individual thought is given to each customer's requirements. The bodies are framed in English Ash, long matured in our timber yard and are built to withstand the strains of the roughest roads.

'We specialise in repairs, re-upholstery, repainting etc and are official repairers to the chief insurance companies.

'It will be hardly fair to go from the Works without making mention of the men. A light and airy mess room is provided together with a kitchen for warming their meals. During the dinner hour the men enjoy a game of football on the ground adjoining the Works, keen rivalry existing between the engineering and body-building shops.

We have found that periodical social gatherings increase the goodwill between employee and employer. During the winter months whist drives and musical evenings are organised and the men spend many a happy hour with their wives and friends.'

Top: Outside the Billacombe Works. Bottom: Inside the Mess Room.

Mumfords appear to be the only company locally who worked on such an industrial scale. They had a large workforce and while they did not manufacture vehicle chassis or engines, they dealt with many of the top marques. It is fascinating to reflect that this meant the main distinguishing feature of any vehicle that rolled out of their workshops was the radiator grille.

With a clear distinction between commercial vehicles and pleasure vehicles, it's worth remembering that back in the mid-1920s when Mumfords produced their anniversary booklet, the leisure market for cars was still relatively limited. Beyond the pocket of most working men, car sales still had a long way to go and motorcycles were the dream machines of the modern man of the time.

The times were changing fast though and the number of cars on the road was increasing substantially year on year and when the opportunity came up in December 1927 to purchase the ailing Abbey Garage of the late Arthur Charles Lempriere Back in St Andrew Street it was readily jumped on by William Mumford. By this stage his third son, Ronald, had also joined the firm and in 1930 Kenneth completed the line up as it stood at the time. All of which afforded father William the opportunity to retire from the motor trade and focus his attention on his new passion – talking pictures, a brand new cinematic development at the end of the 1920s.

As William went into partnership with local cinema proprietor and pioneer Guy Prance so plans were published to demolish the existing Abbey Garage and create a brand new complex on the site.

So it was that on Sunday 10 September 1933 an all new Abbey Garage opened opposite and below the Abbey Hotel and just down from the eastern end of St Andrew's Church.

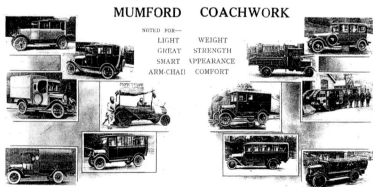

Abbey Garage, St Andrew Street. Left: Images from the 1925 brochure, vehicles include a Great War tank and several of the cars shown on the opposite page.

Clockwise from top left, examples of Mumford's body work: Model T Ford c1918; RAF type Crossley of c1914-16; c1916 English Model T Ford; c1924 35hp Daimler; c1928 20hp Austin hearse; c1924 Fiat (parked outside the Royal Citadel gate on the Hoe).

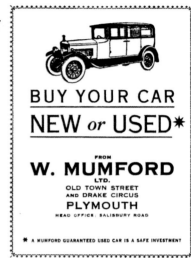

Left: 'For Everything Motorish,' a regular Mumfords strap line in the 1920s. Right: An ad from 1931.

As cars became more affordable and more reliable, so they increased their range to include 'used' cars as well as new ones. One ad from the 1920s ran: 'How much do you wish to spend on a car? Whether it is £50 or £3,000 we can fulfil your requirements in such a way that you will be very satisfied. It is acknowledged that we have the largest and most varied stock of new and used cars in the West, the following being our main agencies:- Daimler, Austin, Rhode, Overland, Singer, Bean, Willys-Knight, Crossley, Falcon-Knight.

'If you buy a new or used car from us you are immediately covered by our AFTER-SALES SERVICE. This is no mere advertising phrase but a real live part of our organisation. Our Service Manager (at our Abbey Garage Depot) will care for your every need and see that your motoring is made a pleasure.'

In addition to the showroom near Drake Circus in Old Town Street a further facility was opened in a very conspicuous location towards the bottom of the street opposite the small park that had been created on part of the old St Andrew's burial yard site in the 1890s.

Top: Upper showroom in Old Town Street. Middle general view of Old Town Street with the showroom on the right. Bottom: The Mumford works in Salisbury Road.

This showroom focussed on the used car market and as we see in the summer of 1937 image opposite, all of their second hand cars here were being sold at less than £50 (around £3,500 today).
It's also interesting to note that on an early 1930s advertisement they felt moved to state that 'a Mumford guaranteed used car is a safe investment'.

H ANDREW & CO

Main image: The new garage at Athenaeum Plac, in the doorway is a c1906 Sizaire Naudin. Top: 1903 Andrew ad for the firm based in Yealmpton. Middle: 1905 Andrew now in Athenaeum Place - opposite Stage Door, Royal Theatre. Bottom: 1909

On Saturday 18 March 1905 an advertisement appeared in the *Western Morning News* giving preliminary notice of the fact that H Andrew & Co, Motor Engineers of Plympton 'will shortly open Extensive Premises at Athenaeum Place, Plymouth (close to the Royal Hotel), where Cars can be Cleaned, Stored, and Repairs undertaken by Certified Mechanics.'

The ad also boasted of a 'large garage' and claimed to be the 'Cheapest House in the West for Accessories.'

Furthermore there was notice of a handful of vehicles they currently had on sale:

'8-9-hp 2-cyclinder Celment-Talbot, new, not yet delivered from the makers £266

10-hp 2-cyclinder Napier, new, £250

3-hp Rexette (1905), new especially upholstered, splendid condition £35

There was also a '2-hp petroleum engine, in perfect condition, nearly new' and 'suitable for electric lighting, governors, water tank, £30 or nearest offer.'

Quite how long H Andrew had been in business by this stage is unclear, but given that he was still only in his 20s in 1905 it is likely that his operations in Yealmpton and his native Plympton were relatively short lived.

Certainly the new garage, given it's proximity to the Theatre Royal and Royal Hotel, was ideal in many ways. The area outside the Theatre entrance was a terminus for trams and before long buses too, so that it was easy for potential clients to find their way to Athenaeum Lane.

Andrew was clearly anxious to tap up the affluent middle classes and an early 1907 ad for the latest Ford described the car as the 'ideal doctor's car, fast and reliable, guaranteed for twelve months,' moreover prospective purchasers could take a trial run at any time.

A few years later the location proved perfect for a rather unusual publicity stunt as one of the Andrew & Co team drove one of the latest Fords up the steps at the western end of the colonnade and down the steps nearest to Derry's Clock.

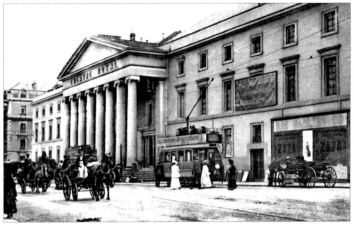

1913: A Ford car owned by H Andrew & Co, Plymouth ascending and descending the steps of the Theatre Royal, Plymouth.

Two shots of Andrew's garage and repair shop from December 1924, which his 1919 advertisement (right) claimed to be the largest and most efficient in the West.

Andrew was clearly one of the more successful of the early Plymouth garage proprietors. Sometime around the end of the Great War he commissioned new workshops and machine rooms on a vacant plot in Athenaeum Place adjacent to his existing garage complex. Soon after they were completed he took over an empty shop in George Street, just across from the Theatre Royal and the George Street junction with Athenaeum Place. It was from here that Andrew started showing off the wide range of marques that he was licensed to sell including the new for 1928 Citroen. This national ad was branded by different local outlets, it tells us a great deal about motoring in 1928!

Left: George Street in the mid-1920s. Andrew opened his showroom here around this time, note the large ad for H Andrew & Co, on the side wall of his building. Above: 1937, two views of his premises in Athenaeum Lane, the top one looking west from Lockyer Street, the bottom looking north towards George Street.

Dear Sirs,

I feel I must write and tell you how awfully pleased I am with the 4-seater Coupé I bought from you last January.

I will admit I bought it mainly for the body! I liked its smart lines and chic appearance – and the ample leg-room (I am 5ft 10ins), also the extra seat which appealed to me on account of the children. In fact, it seemed an ideal car for my purposes – and I wasn't particularly interested in the engine, provided it gave no trouble.

However, from the first its power surprised me, and I thought I should like to try and get to Edinburgh in a day! My friends were amused and sceptical, being of the opinion that it would be too much for a woman to do alone in a 12hp car.

But on Monday week at 4.25 am I set out from my home at Carshalton Beeches and arrived at Edinburgh at 7.10pm, a distance of 416 miles by the route I took. Allowing about one-and-a-quarter hours for meals, filling up, etc, the average works out to about 31 mph, I could have made better going had I not been advised to keep her down below 45 mph.

I had no trouble whatever, had a very pleasant and comfortable journey and was neither physically nor mentally tired at the end of it.' Mrs KBDM

BARTONS, MUTLEY PLAIN

Frank Barton was the son of a London draper, Robert Barton and his dressmaker wife, Sarah. The couple were both originally from Wiltshire, but had moved to Islington where young Frank initially followed the family calling. However, sometime after his 21st birthday he and his younger brother William set up a cycle business in Bridgewater and Taunton.

Barton Brothers styled themselves Cycle Agents and Repairers, but unfortunately a lack of capital investment and an inability to make a success of 'letting out cycles on a hire purchase system' led to the early insolvency of the business in September of 1894. The situation had been compounded by William's decision to enlist in the Army.

Still enthusiastic about the future of wheeled transport, we find Frank, now married to Anne (Pollard), working for the Oxford Cycle Company by 1898. Within a year or two he was back in business in his own right, once again as a 'Cycle Agent and Repairer.'

By this stage he would certainly have been acquainted with another self-made cycle seller and repairer, William Morris. Born in Worcester, Morris's parents had moved to Oxford in 1880 and on leaving school in 1892 he had been apprenticed to a local cycle dealer. Less than a year later, having been refused a pay increase, 16-year-old William set up his own business at the back of his family home. From here he started assembling bicycles as well as repairing them. He also started racing them, including one he called 'The Morris.' He became the local champion cyclist, in Oxford, Berkshire and Buckinghamshire, over distances ranging from one to 50 miles.

In 1901 William began working with motors and designed the Morris Motor Cycle. Business boomed. He hired larger premises and started dealing in the first generation of motor cars. Morris became an agent for Arrol-Johnston, Belsize, Humber, Hupmobile, Singer, Standard and Wolseley.

New premises were erected in Longwall Street and were almost immediately dubbed The Oxford Motor Palace in the local press. Meanwhile William changed the official name of the business from The Oxford Garage to The Morris Garage.

By this stage Frank Barton, who had also been a local cycling champion, had joined Morris as a car salesman. The market was starting to take off and in 1912 William Morris, with input from Frank on design and construction, produced his own vehicle, adapting components imported from the States.

The first 'bullnose' Morris was mass produced in a disused military training college in Cowley, Oxford. Inevitably, production during the 1914-18 war was primarily given over to munitions but in 1919 car production resumed and 400 cars were sold that year.

Around this time Frank Barton, by now Morris's general manager, became quite ill and his doctor suggested a move to a better climate, like that to be found in Devon. And so it was that Frank moved to Torquay, where he opened his first garage in Torwood Street. His second son, Richard, born of his second wife, May (nee Keeler), was born there in October 1918. Happily Frank's health improved and he decided to stay put and open a Morris agency in Plymouth. A couple of weeks before Christmas 1923 an advertisement appeared in the *Western Evening Herald*: 'Morris-Oxford and Morris-Cowley Cars.

'Mr F G Barton has pleasure in announcing that he has opened premises at 54 Mutley-plain, Plymouth, as a Sales and Service Agency for the above popular cars, which represent the finest motor car value to-day. He would emphasize that they are not 6, 7, 8 or even 10 hp, but 11.9, and will go anywhere over the Moors. Morris repairs and spare parts a speciality. Inquiries from agents in Devonshire and East Cornwall invited. Phone 206.'

The new enterprise was an instant success and Bartons weren't at all shy about celebrating their sales stats. In September 1926 Frank took the interesting step of getting a Torquay-based accountant to produce the following affidavit as a piece of advertising:

'I have examined the SALE BOOKS of the BARTON MOTOR COMPANY, LIMITED (Plymouth and Exeter) and I hereby certify that the actual SALE by them of NEW MORRIS CARS (exclusive of all second-hand sales) from 1 September 1925 to 11 March 1926, was 500 (Five Hundred) (signed) C E Riding (Chartered Accountant).'

A post script to the display read 'buy British and be Proud of it.' With the clout of the Morris organisation behind him, and the increasing popularity both of the motor car in general and the

Morris in particular, Barton's job was made that much easier. By 1925 William Morris had built or bought production facilities at Abingdon, Birmingham and Swindon to add to his expanding Oxford operation and such was the level of their success that in 1925 alone Morris sold some 56,000 cars across the UK. Barton's contribution to that stat was relatively substantial and just a few years later they were able to boast by September (1928) that they had sold 1000 cars already that year. Although, admittedly, this was now across their showrooms on Mutley Plain and in Fore Street, Exeter.

Left:1926 ad and a view of 'Morris Corner' on the corner of Mutley Plain and Ford Park. Above: Two views celebrating 1000 cars sold by Bartons in 1928.

1926 Carnival time at Bartons.

These were heady times, the 1920s were a decade of great changes. More and more houses were being hooked up to the electricity network, wireless sets were introducing the newly formed British Broadcasting Company (1922) into people's homes and at the end of the decade sound was being added to the already hugely popular cultural phenomenon of moving pictures. While the Mutley Cinedrome might have closed, the purpose built Belgrave Cinema was experiencing plenty of demand. There was plenty of demand too for Morris motor cars and nationally the company were ahead of the game, employing a creative and innovative advertising campaign to which local dealers simply had to append their own details.

Barton's initial Plymouth Mutley base on the corner of Ford Park had, in 1919, housed John Mumford's Cycle and Perambulator business. Within a few years Bartons had expanded into 56 Mutley Plain, which had previously been the home of the Mutley Cinedrone. John Mumford meanwhile had moved into No58. Five doors along the Plain, towards Hyde Park, Joseph Mumford had the high-street base of the Mumford & Sons motor business. It would appear that the Barton enterprise either shared or existed alongside separate Mumford concerns in Belgrave Lane and Salisbury Road.

Overall there could be little doubt that William Mumford and Frank Barton were emerging as the two main figures in the fast growing local motor trade.

Saturday 5 July 1924: Some of the competitors awaiting the start at West Hoe in the rally of cars manufactured by the Morris Works which took place at Plymouth and Yelverston on Saturday. The event organised by the Barton Motor Co the local distributing agents for Morris cars was unique so far as Devon is concerned.

As the decade advanced so did the sophistication and subtlety of the Morris advertising department, viz this offering from 1928 which was undoubtedly a little dig at the money people were spending at the movies:

Why don't we buy a MORRIS?

'Ask yourself the question once more and consider it in this light. What is your family amusement bill per annum? £30? And railway travelling? £20?

'Think. £35.12s.10d down secures you delivery of a Morris – the balance you pay over twelve or eighteen months. At the end of that time the money you would have spent on fares and amusements has gone into sound investment. Many more years of Morris ownership and pleasure are yet before you – and then a high cash value for your Morris if you wish to sell it or exchange.

'Upkeep costs? The Morris is the cheapest car in the world to run. 1,750 individual Dealer Service Organisations pledged to observe a standardised scale of repair charges, a low tax, extreme economy of petrol, oil and tyres make it so.

'Go into the question thoroughly.

'Send for a Catalogue and full details of Guarantee, Hire Purchase and Service facilities to Enquiries Morris Motors (1926) Ltd, Cowley, Oxford.

Dunlop Tyres Standard

Barton Mutley Plain, Plymouth and Fore Street, Exeter.'

Two years later the message was even more simple as the wording of this 1930 ad, which was set in an eye-catching amount of white space: 'That there are many more Morris Cars on our roads to-day than any other make has a bigger significance than anything else we can tell you.'

Above: Morris ad from 1930. Right: 1928 - illustrations from popular Broadstairs artist Gilbert Rumbold.

Small wonder therefore that Frank Barton was, at the end of the 1920s, in a position to purchase a large site further along Mutley Plain and commission one of the first purpose built motor showrooms in the city.

Indeed it's interesting to note that Plymouth had only just become a city in 1928 and five years later Bartons were advertising their new Morris Car Showrooms as being 'in the Centre of the City.' With steelwork by local contractors Blight & White, the development was overseen by Wakeham Brothers, while the architect for the scheme was H J Hammick.

As part of the outcome of the project a new road was created to the west of the iconic Hyde Park Hotel which, henceforth, was destined to stand alone, on what became an island site at the bottom of Townsend Hill.

With internal ramps connecting the different floors, the new showroom was a state of the art affair with, somewhat unusually for the time, a petrol dispensing facility on its southern elevation. The new showroom was opened on Monday 31 March 1930 by the recently enobled Sir William Morris.

After the ceremony Morris was given a tour of the premises and then entertained at the Royal Hotel, at Derry's Cross where he was presented with a silver replica of Drake's *Golden Hind*.

It was a major event and at it Sir William informed his audience that he would be giving £200,000 (in excess of 13 million today) of profits received by Morris Motors to charitable causes.

Meanwhile Marcus Linz, the son of a Russian sewing machine engineer and a director of Barton's, announced a profit sharing scheme for every member of Barton's staff.

Clearly there would have been smiles all around, with hearty applause for Frank Barton's wife, May, who was presented with a large bouquet of flowers by the company's youngest employee, Miss Pittwood.

With production systems more efficient than ever and cars available from as little as £200 demand was high and Barton's had a bonus for all buyers – all cars came with a free driving lesson! There was as yet no requirement for drivers to have passed a test or for them to display any deep knowledge of an as yet unwritten comprehensive code of conduct for all road users.

Workmen pose precariously as steelwork is erected on the new Barton site.

Vehicles lined up inside and outside the completed structure.

Barton

Barton

Barton
MOTOR COMPANY LIMITED.
"THE LARGEST DEALERS IN THE WEST."
HYDE PARK CORNER, PLYMOUTH.

Above: The impressive new Barton Building at the end of Mutley Plain with an original sign now to be found outside the Hyde Park. Right: An early aerial perspective of the new building.

Above: Opening day at the new showroom on Hyde Park Corner, over 20 Morris cars, a Moth aeroplane and a yacht are among the objects on display.
Right: Sir William Morris, May and Frank Barton at the opening.
Left: March 1933, for the benefit of airmen, following the opening of Plymouth airport at Roborough, a large directional sign guiding airmen to the airfield, is painted on the roof of the Barton building.

In the *Western Morning News* account of the luncheon, Sir William Morris was quoted as saying that he had 'much pleasure in coming to Plymouth, more particularly because it was at the invitation of Mr Barton, who with him started WRM Motors Ltd., at Cowley, Oxford.

'Mr Barton,' he said, 'helped me considerably. We both worked like ni**ers until Mr Barton went back from where I took him. I don't think there is a man in the world who could give Mr Barton a start in selling a motor car. (Laughter.)

'Mr Barton had the reputation that if a man came in for a sparking plug he went out with a motor car!'

Then, having already outlined the difficulties the motor industry faced in the aftermath of the Great War, he said: 'The motor trade in this country is trying to get on its feet again. We are,' he affirmed, 'doing everything we can to bring the old country back to the position it should hold.'

Like Frank Barton, Sir William had started in the cycle trade and he went on to say that 'the whole of England, Scotland, and Wales had been swamped with machines from another country, but today England supplied not only the whole of the British Isles, but the whole of the Dominions. Similarly,' he added, 'in the motor cycle trade today the British machine was supreme. In the colonies the old country would,' he thought, 'rise and regain what it had lost.'

In a special interview with a representative of the *Western Morning News*, Sir William subsequently spoke optimistically of the prospects of the motor trade in its associations with South Africa, where he had recently been a visitor. 'There is certainly scope for expansion of the motor trade in South Africa,' he said, and if we take advantage of our opportunities there are considerable possibilities in that direction.'

Five years later Barton's opened a second hand car showroom in Market Place, Plymouth, followed, in 1937, by the opening of a second garage in Torquay, at Saint Marychurch.

In 1939 Morris, nationally, recorded the sale of their one millionth vehicle!

Right: From 1933, another classic Morris advertisement; the text reads: 'We could have taken out the picture altogether and filled the whole page with type-set enthusiasm ... about the train-de-luxe travel of the '25' or the power of its engine, now indolent, now fleet, or the way great hills just go down before it. Let the '25' explain its own merits to you quietly, effectively ... your local Morris dealer can arrange this ... or write us direct.'

Left: The Morris 8

Above: Three Barton ads from 1939.

Note the three motorcycles parked outside: one wonders if this was where, in May 1939, a lorry belonging to a London firm – Messrs Holden – reversed into one of Pike's motorcycles and was subsequently fined £2.14s.3d. for damages in Plymouth County Court. Note also the faded ad for Raleigh cycles on the facing wall.

P PIKE & CO LIMITED

Philip Pike, the son of an Exeter publican, was one of the biggest names in Plymouth's motor cycle trade before the war.

It appears that Philip started out in Exeter, as a young man working as a cycle merchant's traveller before setting up his own 'Motor Cycle and Cycle Car Works'. In 1911, the year after his mother died, he married Daisy Louise Heale, from Torquay and by 1919 was operating out of premises in Alphington Street, St Thomas, Exeter. These were still the early days of motoring and P Pike & Co promoted 'repairs and tuning' as a speciality.

By 1920, 33-year-old Pike had established premises in Plymouth, in Chapel Street, and the following year he had 'acquired and become successor' to the business of the Exeter Motor Cycle and Light Car Company of Bath Road, Exeter.

A pioneer in the motor trade locally, on 25 May 1935, a Saturday, Philip Pike hosted the start of the fifth annual Riley '24' event. Organized and promoted by the Riley Motor Club the event was designed to be a test of 'average driving skill, reasonable endurance and accepted modern car efficiency'. Plymouth was evidently the only Westcountry starting control out of the 20 or so around the country and the premises here, 166 Union Street, was that very control point.

Late in the summer of 1939 war was declared and the Government were appealing for motorcycles to help with the war effort. The appeal was made through the Press and via the wireless and throughout Devon and Cornwall private owners and dealers were invited to communicate with Pike's as 'regional buyers' before submitting any machines that came up to the War Office specifications.'

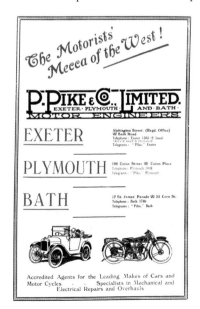

Phil Pike was also an eminent member of the Plymouth Motor Club whose HQ was in the Farley Hotel, opposite Pike's premises in Union Street. Right: Ads from 1926 and 1938.

Phil Pike cigarette in hand, pictured on his Norton in Union Street, in September 1924 part way through his epic bike ride, opposite his shop premises with his daughter Phyllis alongside with his 'official observer' Mr Bourne from the Auto-Cycle Union in the side car.

PHIL PIKE'S EPIC BIKE RIDE

On the 24 September 1924 just three weeks after his 37th birthday, Phil Pike, passed through Plymouth on quest to ride from Land's End to John O'Groats and back ... twice. He also intended to run his bike up and down Porlock Hill – the steepest stretch of A-road in the country – 20 times at the end of the ordeal so that he could register a total journey of 4060 miles. Clearly this was no walk in the park and in order to ensure that he didn't cut any corners or tamper unduly with his machine, he was accompanied by an official observer from the ACU (Auto Cycle Union).

The ACU had been founded some 20 years earlier as the Auto-Cycle Club – an offshoot of the Automobile Club of Great Britain. In 1907 both organisations were renamed, as the former became the Auto-Cycle Union and the latter was restyled the Royal Automobile Club (RAC). Since 1924, the year Mr Bourne sat in Pike's motor-cycle side car for mile after mile, the ACU has been focussed entirely on promoting and controlling the sport and pastime of motorcycling.

To that end there can be little doubt that Pike's self imposed challenge was one that would inevitably generate great interest in the rapidly rising popularity of the motor-cycle, more specifically the Norton. Produced by a Birmingham-based company that had been started up by James Lansdowne ('Pa') Norton back in 1898. Pike's drop into Plymouth came after he'd already been on the road nine days and at that stage he was 'very little behind his scheduled time, and taking into consideration the arduous nature his undertaking, he bore few signs the strenuous task.'

The local press further reported that 'a knot of motor cycle enthusiasts gathered to greet the rider in Plymouth, having first ensured that everything in the way of the replenishment fuel was ready for him, and when he and his companion put in an appearance smiling and cheery, cheers went up.

Everything was going all right, said Mr. Pike, and the only complaint he had was against the weather: "It has been simply atrocious, end we have experienced floods in certain places."

'Yesterday they had had to contend with violent wind, which was the cause of their being behind time, as well as the fact that no allowance was made for meal times or replenishing fuel. He was, however, "feeling fit as a fiddle," and had no trouble with the machine.

'Mr. Pike left Land's End on September 15 and, travelling via Gloucester, Birmingham, Warrington, Carlisle, Stirling, Inverness, and Wick, reached his northernmost point September 19, averaging about 250 miles per day. Up to the time of reaching Plymouth yesterday he had completed 1,791 miles.

'Did the rest of the journey go as smoothly? Yes, almost ... but not entirely. After reaching Land's End for the final time, Pike and Bourne headed off to Porlock Hill for the final trials.

'They were 55 miles shy of the end of their epic journey, when, at Chudleigh Knighton a charabanc came out of the Bovey Tracey road and collided with the dynamic duo. Both men were shaken but not injured, however the Norton combination was badly damaged and they were unable to complete their mission there and then.

'A new frame was fitted to the machine, and the tests were completed on the Saturday. When on Porlock Hill, Pike performed his 20 successive climbs on schedule. On the 20th ascent he attained 21 miles per hour up the hill. The engine when dismantled proved singularly free from carbon, and there was no play in the bearings.

'Fortunately the unfortunate charabanc accident was not adjudged to have impaired the value of the trial, as the engine and sealed tank had not been touched.'

AC TURNER AUSTIN DEALER

On Wednesday 13 February 1935 the photograph on p137 appeared in the *Western Morning News* and *Daily Gazette* and the text that accompanied it gives us a wonderful insight into the state of the motor industry in Plymouth at that time.

'In 1909 Mr A C Turner started a garage in Gibbon-lane, Plymouth. Sales were two or three a year and trade was mostly repair and hire work with a car or two. Today Messrs A C Turner and Co. Ltd. have a contract for the sale of 603 Austin cars, have eight Austin landaulets on constant hire, and employ 25 people on full-time pay.

'This, in brief, symbolises the growth of a modern firm, built up on personal service, and the great strides made in the motoring industry. The years have marked constant advance, culminating in the establishment of modern showrooms. Always, however, the personal 'touch' has been maintained.

'After four years at Gibbon Lane Mr Turner moved to the premises at 13 Tavistock Road, and in 1919 he became Austin distributor, signing a contract for 20 cars. With the distributing of the 600 Austins this year Messrs. Turner, who became a limited company in 1923, have an area to serve including the immediate district up to Tavistock, and the areas around Liskeard, St Austell, Bodmin, and Wadebridge.

'A large service depot is maintained at Kirkby Place, only two minutes from their showrooms, where all repairs can be executed. Every spare part for Austin cars is available. Some £2,000 worth of spares being constantly in stock.

'Some idea of the growth of popularity of Austin cars, and proof of the contention that an Austin is an investment' can be gained from some of the contracts secured by Messrs. Turner during the last 18 months. The Western National Omnibus Co., Ltd. have purchased a fleet of 18 Austins for their inspectors: Plymouth St John Ambulance have six Austin ambulances: a similar number of vehicles have been formed into a fleet by the Plymouth and Stonehouse Gas Light and Coke Co: and the city police this month will be taking four Austins.

'Messrs Turner have also witnessed another feature in connection with the growth of the motor industry. In 1923 the Austin Co. introduced the first 'baby' car. It cost over £160 and was a tourer. It proved an instant success and today of Messrs Turner's contract of 603 Austins no fewer than 300 are for "babies". There is a two-seater at £100 and a saloon, with sliding roof at £120.

'When they first started with Austin cars Messrs Turner had only one model for sale, the famous '20.' Today there are nine models of private cars, ranging from the '7' to the '20' and six standardized commercial types, while any special body, such as for ambulances, can be obtained.'

The feature also went into great detail concerning the showroom itself, a showroom incidentally that many old Plymothians may well recall as it survived the war and stood for many years after that: 'Modern in every aspect, the new show-rooms of Messrs AC Turner and Co. Ltd., in Tavistock Road, Plymouth, occupy an imposing position, and the clean and neat building will improve the appearance of the corner.

A 'Baby' Austin.

1924 An AC Turner charabanc outing to Paignton.

The distinctive triangular shape of the AC Turner building.

'Messrs. Turner will be using their new premises solely for the display of Austin cars, for which they are the distributors, and the present premises at 13, Tavistock Road will be utilized for spare parts and a selection of second hand cars will also be kept there. The present plan is to use only the ground floor of the new showrooms, the outstanding feature of which is the window space. Triangular in shape, the rooms have two long window-lengths coming to an apex, the base of the triangle being only about one-third of the part of the showroom, for the windows are of the modern type with small joining pillars to give maximum lighting. As the premises are not 'closed in' by surrounding buildings, the showroom will have little need of artificial illumination except at night and during the very dark days.

'This glass was supplied to the shopfitters by Messrs J M Newton and Andrewartha, of Plymouth.

'Room will be provided for at least 20 cars, with plenty of space to inspect each one, while the flooring is of the parquet type. All the woodwork is in oak and there are two big sliding doors for easy exit and entrance of cars, Messrs. Harris and Sons having been responsible for the shopfitting.

'Lighting is provided by movable flood electric reflectors, a large number of which have been installed by Messrs. Brewer and Phillips, of Plymouth, while neon lighting, for which Messrs. F Ford and Co. Ltd., of Exeter, have been responsible, has been utilized for outside display.

'Blinds have been fixed to every window by Messrs. Wakeham Bros.; the steelwork has been provided by Messrs. Blight and White Ltd.; the Western Counties Brick Co. have been responsible for the bricks. The architects were Messrs. Barron and Rooke, of Plymouth.'

Above: AC Turner's Austin House in Tavistock Road.
Right: Colyn Thomas's Austin 7.

'Sir Herbert Austin in Plymouth at a lunch in the Duke of Cornwall Hotel, to celebrate the opening of the new show-rooms of Messrs AC Turner on 15 April 1935. Among those present and seated on the top table: Alderman Solomon Stephens, Mr AC Turner, Mr WHJ Priest, Mr HE Turner and Sir Herbert Austin.'

Arthur C Turner was the youngest son of the Reverend Charles Edgar Turner, the Vicar of St Edward's Church, Eggbuckland, for over 40 years. Arthur was born in 1888 and left school at the age of 16 and was apprenticed to WJ Andrew, of Andrew's Garage, Plymouth.

An early 'petrol head,' on Monday 15 June 1908, young Arthur was, with fellow motor engineer Herbert Smiles, driving down Old Town Street at what was alleged to be a speed that was dangerous to the public.

At that time there were very few cars going around the Three Towns and Herbert was pulled up by Police Constable Lake and summoned to appear in court the following day.

PC Lake said that at 7.55pm he saw a motor car come from Ebrington Street through Old Town Street travelling at a rate of over 20 miles an hour. People had to 'fly' out of its way. At 9.45pm he again saw the motor car near Drake's Circus and it was then going at a dangerous rate. PC Lake held up his hands and Smiles pulled up within 20 yards, whereupon he was informed that his driving was very dangerous. Fellow police officer, PC Burner, said that as the thoroughfare was crowded, the speed was altogether too fast: 'It must have been 17 miles an hour,' he claimed.

Herbert however claimed that he was only travelling at six or seven miles an hour. The top speed of the car, he averred, was 45 miles an hour, but that could only be on a completely clear road. The retort came 'If the car can go 45mph on a clear road, why not 17mph in Old Town Street?'

To which Mr Smiles replied: 'It is impossible with all the traffic there.' Arthur Turner concurred: as the passenger in the car he said the speed was not more than seven miles an hour. The case was dismissed.

There were of course no speed cameras in those days ... and speedometers didn't become standard fittings in motor cars until a few years later. Meanwhile, one year later, Arthur Turner established his own garage business in Gibbon Lane. At that time work was mainly repair and car hire and car sales were around two or three cars a year.

Four years later though he opened new premises at 13 Tavistock Road, with extensive workshops in Kirkby Place, across from the James Street Vaults.

In 1919 Arthur became the Austin distributor for Plymouth and East Cornwall serving an area up to Tavistock and across the Tamar into Cornwall as far down as St Austell and Wadebridge. Sales boomed and in 1923 Messrs Turner became a limited company.

In 1934 Arthur acquired numbers 48 and 49 Tavistock Place, along with No1 Clarence Street which ran into Tavistock Place and where the new premises were erected.

The new facility was opened on 15 April 1935 by Sir Herbert Austin, founder of the Austin motor car company. At a luncheon afterwards in the Duke of Cornwall Hotel, hosted by Arthur Turner, Sir Herbert expressed his approval of the measures recently introduced by the then Minister of Transport, who was also the sitting MP for Devonport, Leslie Hore-Belisha. Drawing a parallel between road and rail, Sir Herbert said there needed to be separate roads for motorists: 'You do not find cattle, pigs, poultry, or old men walking about in the rails (train lines) ... we cannot allow the cyclist, the pedestrian or farmer to use the roads

A selection of ads from 1939 for the lastest range of Austins.

just as they wish without taking notice of the fact that they are covered with fast-moving vehicles. We must look at least 25 years ahead.'

Hore Belisha's new legislation introduced a 30mph speed limit, new road crossing points (hence what became known as Belisha Beacons) and the introduction of the driving test.

Sir Herbert also paid compliment to the roads in Plymouth, which he described as 'better than in some cities.' He also expressed pleasure at the fact that Messrs. Turners' business had expanded over 50% during the previous year.

Responding, Arthur Turner, honouring his guest, said 'wherever in the world a motor car was known, the name of Sir Herbert Austin was known. By his incessant energy and perseverance he has made the Austin car what it is today.'

DAVIS' GARAGE

It was during the last decade of the nineteenth century that 30-something Richard Frank Davis set up a business as a watchmaker in Treville Street, just off Old Town Street. The son of a local railway guard, Richard, somewhat unusually, added 'cycle agent' to his business model and then, in the first decade of the twentieth century expanded his operations to enter the burgeoning motor trade. Retaining his Treville Street operation he opened 'The Garage' in a former cabinet maker's premises at 20-21 Buckwell Street. Trading initially as The Plymouth Automobile Engineering Company Ltd, in 1906 he was offering 'instruction to NCOs (Non Commissioned Officers) and Men of HM Government via a series of Theoretical and Practical Classes suitable for obtaining the Automobile Club's Certificate.'

The following year he was advertising himself as the sole agent in Devon and Cornwall for Belsize cars.

Named after Marshall & Co's, Belsize Works in Manchester, the company had then been going ten years and were one of the first car manufacturers in the UK. Based on the French Hurtu cars (which in turn were based on the early Benz), the Belsize brand was consolidated in 1906 when the company changed the name to Belsize Motors.

At that time they were major players in the home market employing 1,200 people and producing up to 50 cars a week. As supplied by RF Davis these cars came 'complete with all lamps, tools etc.' and were therefore 'ready for the road.'

Davis himself meanwhile appeared to be ready for anything. In addition to his motoring interests, his cycling and watchmaking skills had seen him act as time-keeper for the National Cyclists Union world championships held in Plymouth and Exeter in 1903 and 1907. He was timekeeper for all the motor cycle racing held at Home Park and was a judge at the Olympic games held at the Stadium, London, in 1908.

His expertise in the art of timekeeping also saw him make numerous court appearances on behalf of men and women accused by the local constabulary of speeding offences.

Although we have few details the business clearly prospered and before long a couple of his sons, Percy and Reginald, had entered the business and by 1921 another garage had been opened this time in the rapidly expanding heart of Crownhill.

Located in Morshead Road, just north of the Tamar Hotel, the Crownhill property was evidently built as a chapel, and had since become a forage merchant's store and then a dame school.

The property would long come to be associated with R F Davis jnr – that is Reginald Fletcher Davis (his middle name being his mother's maiden name and his father dying in 1927). The phone number of the new enterprise incidentally was Crownhill 4.

  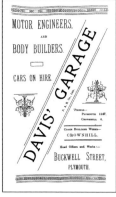

Left: and far right: Davis Garage ads from 1921. Middle: View of what was then Widey Terrace c1921, note the Crownhill Telephone Exchange on right and garage by the car.

Top left: Early aerial of Crownhill c1920s. Right: Later view of Davis Garage in Morshead Road, telephone no 71124. Above: c1925 view of the Davis garage (far right, note the Pratt pertrol pump), Tamar Hotel and Police Station. CO 6435 is a two seater Fiat, registered in February 1924 to A W Ross of 21 Clarendon Place, on the Hoe.

SNELLS MOTOR HOUSE

Frank Snell was born in Chudleigh in 1864 and became an apprentice wheelwright before he left home. He came to Plymouth in the late 1880s and set up as a wheelwright in Cambridge Street. One of the first to embrace cycle manufacture locally, Frank clearly had an eye to whatever the next big thing might be, he also had a fascination for things that went round and round. By 1906 he had moved his operation to 'newly-built, commodious premises' in Frankfort Buildings which sat opposite the southern end of Cambridge Street. Here the enterprising Mr Snell was selling cycles, tyres, phonographs, gramophones and BSA rifles (BSA, the Birmingham Small Arms Company were also pioneering motor cycle manufacturers so there was an obvious enough link).

In an advertisement in the *Western Evening Herald* that year – the ad, incidentally, was one column wide and ran from the top to the bottom of the page – he boasted that they would make 'unceasing efforts in every trading action to yield the patrons of our trade the fullest satisfaction.' The ad was top and tailed with the strapline 'Facts worth telling and goods worth selling.'

Snell advertised regularly and clearly his approach had something to commend it. Ten years later we find him using the same medium to inform potential patrons that 'Frank Snell, Frankfort Street, Motor and Cycle Engineer, having completed his new Motor Garage in St Andrew Street is prepared to submit estimates for OVERHAULING, REPAINTING, and RE-UPHOLSTERING any kind of Motor or Sidecars, RECOVERING HOODS A Speciality.'

He then added, for the benefit of anyone who might be in doubt: 'ONLY EXPERIENCED WORKMEN EMPLOYED.'

S N E L L S

MOTOR HOUSE

The House for New and Second-hand Bargains

AUSTIN AND TRIUMPH CARS

SUNBEAM, TRIUMPH, B.S.A., ROYAL ENFIELD
SCOTT, JAMES, FRAMIS BARNETT AND O.K. SUPREME

MOTOR CYCLES

Largest Stockist in the West

Easiest of Easy Payments
SECOND-HAND MOTOR CYCLES FROM £5
Don't forget we guarantee our Second-hand Bargains

CALL, PHONE OR WRITE WITHOUT OBLIGATION
Demonstration Runs given without annoyance

NOTE OUR ADDRESSES

Showrooms : 97 Old Town St.
Second-hand Depot : 36 St. Andrew's St.   **PLYMOUTH**
Cycle Dept. : 1 Frankfort Buildings

PHONE 1706   PRAM TYRES

TRIUMPH
2.77 H.P. MODEL W. DE LUXE.

EBRINGTON SKATING RINK,

G. JONES, Proprietor

ADMIT BEARER Monday Evening, 27th Feb., 1911.

High Class ROLLER SKATING.

Allow Bearer use of **Pair of Skates.** Monday, 27th Feb.

Always go to SNELL'S for Cycles and Repairs.

Snell's Motor House, Plymouth

FOR ALL **B.S.A.** PRODUCTS

All B.S.A. Scout Cars in stock Ready to Drive away. Your present model taken in Part Exchange at Full Market Price and the balance can be spread over 12, 18, 24 or 36 months. Let us give you our quotation. Large selection of used cars at all times. New B.S.A. Prices from £168.

Our stock of B.S.A. Motor Cycles want no introducing. We can give immediate delivery of any model. Best Price for your present model and the balance to suit your convenience. Before purchasing your New Model see Snell's quotation. Huge selection of second-hand models always in stock.

B.S.A. 350 S.V. B 23 Standard £46 10s.

Britain's finest Cycle without doubt and every model can be had immediate. We finance our own Hire Purchase so you have no waiting or Collectors. Let us supply you with your new cycle. 50 second-hand Models always in Stock. Prices from £5 10s.

B.S.A. LIGHT TOURIST

Easy Terms to suit every Purchaser. Sellers of B.S.A.'s for 40 yrs.

95-99 OLD TOWN ST. & 1 FRANKFORT BUILDINGS
Telephone 3706   PLYMOUTH   Telegrams—" Tyres "

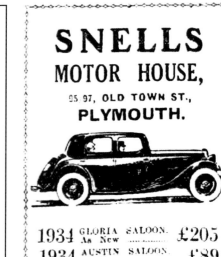

SNELLS
MOTOR HOUSE,
95 97, OLD TOWN ST.,
PLYMOUTH.

1934	GLORIA SALOON. As New	**£205**
1934	AUSTIN SALOON. As New	**£89**
1933	STANDARD BIG NINE SALOON	**£110**
1932	MORRIS TWO-SEATER	**£39/10**

50 USED MOTOR CYCLES FROM £5

SEND FOR LISTS AND TERMS.

**EVERY MODEL GUARANTEED.
NEW CARS IN STOCK.
AUSTIN, MORRIS, AND TRIUMPH.**

SNELLS,
PLYMOUTH.

For his telegram address Snell had managed to obtain the very simple 'Tyres' Plymouth.

A few years later we find Frank Snell embracing another wheeled form of propulsion – roller skates. Initially it would appear that he had some role in sponsoring the activity locally, but then, in 1912, he is listed as being the proprietor of The Rink, in Ebrington Street ... and offering 20 prizes for Spectators and Skaters. Skating was then enjoying its heyday and there were three sessions every day, with 'delightful music and perfect floor.' Particularly popular with young people, this was a wonderful way to appeal to the generation that were most likely to become motor cycle and car owners.

Interestingly, from the late 1920s and right through the 1930s Mrs Snell presented the Snell Trophy at the annual Plymouth Motor Club motorcycle jamboree, latterly for 'solo motorcycles with standard tyres.'

In the 1930s Snell's Motor House opened showrooms in No95, 96, and 97 (and later 99 as well) Old Town Street, in addition to their presence at No1 Frankfort Street, 35, 36, 37 St Andrew Street and out at Arnold's Point on Embankment Road.

*Top left: 1911 ad for The Rink in Ebrington Street - always go to Snell's.
Right top 1939 ad and far right an ad from 1935. Right: Snell's sign
just visible to the side of the impressive Jacobean property at No33.*

1922: Hedley Piper and friend in an Alvis.

HEDLEY PIPER

1921: Hedley Piper in a three-wheel Morgan Sports.

Hedley John Piper had not long turned 20 when these pictures were taken. The earliest record we have for him is as the Honorary Secretary of the Tavistock and District Motor Cycle and Light Car Club in 1922 where he was involved in an organised hill climb event at Lamerton.

The following year the Walkhampton-born farmer's son was running Piper's Garage in Athenaeum Lane, opposite the Theatre Royal in Plymouth and not far from Andrew's already well-established business in Athenaeum Place. Hedley's business never appears to have grown all that much and a succession of minor court cases suggests he was always looking to cut corners in his bid to drive forward his enterprise.

Although quite possibly well-intentioned, his long record suggests a somewhat cavalier attitude to paper-work and provides an interesting insight into the time in which he was operating.

In March 1928 he was fined four shillings, including costs, at Plymouth Police Court for using a motor car 'for which no Road Fund Licence was in force'. He was also fined £3 for a similar offence in respect of a lorry. Apprehended on 21 February for that particular charge, Piper alleged that the vehicle was not used until 20 February and that he had taken out the Road Fund Licence on 22 February.

Two years later he was in court again, and fined 20 shillings (£1 or around £70 today) for the same offence. He claimed he was driving the car to his garage to resell it.

On Tuesday 9 May 1933 he was summoned to court in Tiverton for causing 'a motor car to be used without having in force, in relation to the user, a policy of insurance in respect of third party risk.'

This time Piper was fined £10 with costs of £4.6s.6d (almost £15 altogether – which would translate to around £1000 today).

Piper was represented in court by local Plymouth solicitor John Eliott and eight previous convictions were mentioned including those listed above and another for causing obstruction and one for 'driving a car to the public danger.'

One suspects that once again he was not unduly bothered by any of this ... much to his own cost as it would appear that, on the way back from Tiverton, Piper's sports car hit a bank on a double bend near Burn Halt, about three miles from Bickleigh. In the car with him were his solicitor, Eliott and William Holloway a colleague with whom he shared an address in Leigham Street.

All three men were taken to Tiverton Hospital. Holloway, having sustained only cuts and abrasions was subsequently discharged but Piper and Eliott were detained, the former having fractured his skull, the latter having sustained concussion and severe injuries to both legs. The car, incidentally, was extensively damaged.

Piper's condition was described as 'serious' and it took some time to recover and almost a week later the hospital said he was 'getting on fairly well.'

Be that as it may, it seems that he didn't go back into the car trade and his garage, which had by then moved to 16 North Street, was taken over by Charles Patch.

CAR SALES

At the beginning of the 1930s Percy Fletcher, who was himself in his early thirties, became chairman of the newly constituted board of the 16-strong board of Plymouth Speedway Supporters Club. Clearly an avid fan he was there throughout the decade, through the ups and downs of the sport locally.

In early 1939, Percy and his business partner, Gerald Shobrook, a motor engineer, conspired to launch a private company, Car Sales (Plymouth) Limited, which was set up to buy out their joint venture in Raleigh Street and build on it. Registering the business as a private company, on Saturday 1 April they announced their intention to raise £5,000 by releasing 5,000 shares at £1 each. Later that same month they took delivery of a dozen Morris Ten de Luxe models for use in their 'hire and drive yourself' department. The cars were bought from Barton's on Mutley Plain and it's thought that this was the first time in the West of England that a fleet of new cars had been bought with the sole purpose of hiring them out ... without drivers. The cars, it was said, incidentally, were chosen on 'account of their comfort, reliability and economy.'

Following the declaration of war in September 1939 it wasn't long before blackout regulations came in and a pattern had emerged by which fewer country motorists were using Car Sales' parking facilities and those that were, were moving their cars out of town earlier and earlier. Whereas Car Sales used to be open until 11pm by November 1939 most people had moved their cars out by 6.30 or 7pm.

Fletcher and Shobrook's original plan had been to provide Plymouth with a new car sales facility with additional equipment, facilities for garaging, servicing and repairs. To that end they acquired a site just off Union Street, then a main arterial road through the city. The precise location was Summerland Place, and work had still to be completed when war was declared. The first, but by no means final phase was completed during the first year of hostilities, but the building by then had been requisitioned by the Admiralty and adapted as a stores facility. It continued in that role throughout the war – 'a valuable acquisition for the wartime effort.'

For his part, Percy Fletcher remained in Plymouth throughout the war, and in 1942 he was promoted to sergeant in the Mobile Section of the traffic department of the City Police. In that capacity Percy had driven thousands of miles in total around the town, particularly in the air raids and under blackout conditions, all without accident.

Happily the building came through the war unscathed – quite remarkable considering the chaos visited upon the area all around it during the Blitz.

Sadly Gerald Shobrook was not so fortunate. Five years younger than his business partner, Gerald was 35 when the war started and the young motor engineer had been quick to join the Royal Army Service Corps. Almost immediately he was captured while on active service in France and became a prisoner of war. He died in captivity from an illness in Munich, on 9 June 1941, just months after the Luftwaffe's aerial bombardment had wreaked so much havoc on his home town.

1922 Percy Fletcher in a Vuaxhall Racer.

DRIVING THE KING'S DOCTOR

William Henry Nicholas was born at the very dawn of the twentieth century, in February 1900. Fifteen years later, in the same month that he celebrated his birthday, he signed up for a four-year apprenticeship with Snell's Motors in King Street. However with just under a year to serve, young William, joined the fledgling Royal Naval Air Service. That was on 8 March 1918, the last year of the Great War. A little over three weeks later the RNAS became the Royal Air Force.

William Nicholas was to remain in the service, at RAF Mount Batten, until he was discharged almost eight years to the day after joining – on 7 March 1926. There at the same time as the celebrated Aircraftsman Shaw (aka Ross and born into the world as Thomas Edward Lawrence 'Lawrence of Arabia'), William Nicholas's extended stay in the RAF saw him released from his apprenticeship with Snell's.

Thus it was that on leaving the RAF in 1926, William took up a position as chauffeur to Dr AB Soltau of No1 the Crescent, or Crescent Mansions, as it was then styled (the Nicholas family themselves lived across the road from Millbay Station, just along from the Duke of Cornwall).

Dr Alfred Betram Soltau was no ordinary medic: the son of a nonconformist Plymouth minister, Soltau was a highly sought-after figure who among many other positions held included was physician to King George V. William's work entailed driving the eminent doctor to patients here and there across the country. Most of this was done in Dr Soltau's American Buick which he kept garaged at Athenaeum Street. The good doctor also had an Essex and Clyno.

Soltau had been a brilliant student and had a first class degree from the University of London, but he chose to practise in Plymouth where his family had lived for several generations.

Interested in local politics and military medicine, he was the first commanding officer of the 2nd Wessex Field Ambulance and was appointed physician to the War Office in 1918 and to the Ministry of Pensions for cases of gas poisoning.

He was mentioned in despatches four times and was decorated with the CMG in 1916 and CBE in 1919.

Soltau was gazetted honorary physician to the King in 1925, the year before William Nicholas was taken on as his chauffeur. Dr Soltau however died on 26 July 1930, in London, aged 54. And so, just as the Buick wasn't Dr Soltau's only motorcar so Dr Soltau wasn't the only client that William chauffeured for, as, somewhat impressively, W H Nicholas also drove for the Minister of Transport, Devonport MP, Leslie Hore Belisha, and Lord and Lady Astor, often driving to and from the Astor country home at Cliveden.

In later years William also worked for R Humm Motors on the corner of Westwell Street and Princess Square … and later for Fox & Elliott.

Dr Alfred Betram Soltau's Buick pictured in Athenaeum Street. late 1920s.

Top: c1925 work progresses on the new showroom for Reeds' Garage in Cobourg Street. Above: Cobourg Street not long after the completion of the Reeds' new facility.

REEDS

At Reeds' Annual Dinner and Dance held on Friday 25 February 1938, the company's sales manager, RG Atkinson, delivered a 'witty and able speech' in which he 'traced the growth of the Ford car from the "bone-shaker" of many years ago to the fast streamlined automobile of today.

'The firm of Reeds,' he noted, 'has been a landmark in the Plymouth motor trade for over 20 years.'

He then added, 'The name of Ford is very dear to us and represents all that is best in the motoring world.'

Reeds had indeed been Plymouth's main Ford dealers for many years. They appear to have started out in Stuart Road and Pennycomequick and to have moved up to Cobourg Street around 1924, when Pennycomequick was being redeveloped.

It's interesting to note that in the summer of 1932 proposals were put forward 'with the object of relieving the congestion of traffic in the main business thoroughfares of the city' that one of the streets the Plymouth Watch Committee looked to authorise for car parking was the stretch of Cobourg Street from Reeds to 'opposite Brown's Garage (north side).'

The eldest of six sons born to Willoughby and Lavinia Reed, William Shopland Reed was by then in his mid-60s and had stepped down from the running of the firm. His brother Charles, had started out with a garage in nearby York Place but later, like his father, ran a pub – the Lopes Arms at Roborough.

William's son Gilbert, then in his late-20s, took on the firm with Charles Thriscott as the company's managing director. However Gilbert's ability to get around was hampered somewhat at that time by a two-year suspension of his driving licence after having been found guilty at Torquay Police Court, earlier that month of 'driving a motor-car in a manner dangerous to the public.' The alleged offences had taken place in Abbey Road, Torquay on Boxing Day, 1937.

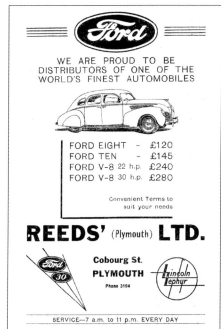

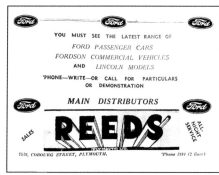

Top: 1937, Spooner's Corner at the bottom of Old Town Street – the bus on the left is sporting a large advertisement for Reeds' while on the far right we see Mumford's second hand car showroom. Left and above: Two 1938 advertisements for Reeds' and their latest Fords.

149

1937, Allen's Garage in Whiteladies Road, Bristol with a display of their new range of Armstrong Siddeley saloons.

ALLENS

C Allen & Son was a rare early example in Plymouth of a motor-car business that wasn't indigenous to the city.

The Allen enterprise had actually been established a century before the arrival of the motor-car in this country, back in 1796, in Taunton. There, Charles Allen senior established a modest enterprise as 'engineers, iron and brass founders and agricultural machinists' at Tone Bridge. From there they manufactured and supplied portable vertical steam engines from one to 12hp, along with boilers and fire-boxes.

They also undertook to make or repair 'every description of agricultural machinery without delay.'

At some point, early in the twentieth century they became motor agents and in 1924 Allens opened an outlet in the then vacant 16 Tavistock Road, a few doors down from AC Turner's showroom. Before long they had opened a second establishment in Tavistock Road, this time in what was the relatively new redbrick block below the Central Library.

The firm also opened an outpost in Whiteladies Road in Bristol, and then in October 1930 a press announcement in the *Western Morning News* informed readers that: 'A block of property in Park Street, Plymouth, including Kinton Hall and the Plymouth Girls' Evening School has been purchased by Messrs C. Allen and Son Ltd., with a view to development.

'Nos. 41-44 Park Street inclusive, comprises three dwelling houses, a shop, the Girls' Evening School, Kinton Hall and a yard at the rear reaching back to Ebrington Street. No definite decision as to how the property is to be utilized will be reached for a week or ten days but the likelihood is that a large garage and car park will be built on the site.'

The site was indeed developed by Allens but they retained the base at 105 Tavistock Road. The Plymouth operation was managed for Allens by George Weeks. The firm sold many well known marques including Vauxhalls, Armstrong Siddeleys and Daimlers, notably, in 1937, the new Daimler 15 Saloon fitted with an 18-guinea radio set.

Top: The lower part of Tavistock Road, with Park Street the first turning to the right. Bottom: 1937 Allens in Whiteladies Road, Bristol, with a general Singer van with a state of the art tow vehicle. The white panel between the windows mentions the Taunton and Plymouth branches.

PEVERELL GARAGE

Wilson Dyer was a former china clay merchant from St Stephens in Cornwall. He came to Plymouth around the time of the Great War and by 1919 had begun operating a garage and a taxi service from his home at 114 Peverell Park Road.

Within a year or two he'd added a couple of lock up garages to his operation and in September 1924, together with a fellow motor engineer called Crowther and Richard Crawshaw, who was to be the company secretary, he floated Peverell Garage Ltd with a move to raise £6000 capital in £1 shares.

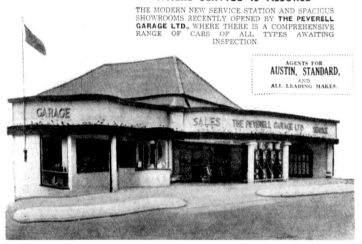

1938 advertisement for the Peverell Garage.

The stated purpose of the new enterprise was 'To acquire the business carried on by W Dyer, at Plymouth and elsewhere, and to carry on the business of motor and general engineers and manufacturers, garage and taxi cab proprietors, mechanical and general transport and commission agents, metal workers, carriers of passengers and goods etc.'

The base of the new business was in Weston Park Road, adjacent to the Peverell Assembly Hall. At that point in time these were the only properties listed as being in Weston Park Road, also known then as the 'High Road' and earlier Mutley Lane, connecting Peverell Park Road to Tavistock Road (presumably Peverell Park Road itself was the 'Low Road').

The Peverell Assembly Hall was a popular concert hall and dance venue for a brief period between then and 1931 when the lease was apparently relinquished. Shortly afterwards the Hall became a car showroom and in 1934 an advertisement informed all that in the second week of May 'Plymothians will have their first opportunity of seeing the new "MG Midget P" type of car.' The ad also mentioned that the newspaper cartoonist Dollery would be there exhibiting his caricatures.

A few years later new showrooms were opened here, and by the late 1930s the garage had become a recognised outlet for Austin, Standard and Hillman cars. All cars costing more than £50 were guaranteed! They had an Austin 7 on sale for £40 and another for £55.

Two of Wilson Dyer's sons, John Henry and Gordon were destined to follow their father into the motor trade and in 1929, when he was just 28, John Henry, in a manner typical of young men with access to 'fast' cars, was fined £1 by Saltash magistrates for 'driving a motor car in a manner dangerous to the public.'

FOLLAND

'My grandfather, William George Folland, started the business back in 1892,' recalled Arthur Folland, of Wembury. He dealt in oil at first, operating out of No11 Florence Place, Embankment Road – he had a stable at the back of the property for the horse. Just before the First World War my father, also William George, took the business on and they moved into what used to be a Home Guard hut for defending Laira bridge in the event of attack. It was a shocking place inside, but father bought the site, along with the old toll houses there. There was also armament depot there behind the 'dockyard' wall. My mates and I used to play in there when we were young.

'Originally the petrol pumps were mounted on the wall, then we had the more modern free-standing pumps right on the roadside. Later the council would try and move us way back off the road again, both to stop the congestion caused by people stopping for petrol and because they wanted to widen the road.'

1912 William George Folland senior with WGF junior on the cart.

Folland's Garage, Laira Bridge, left to right Butcher and his van from Grenville Road, William George Folland, William jnr.

TAMBLINS, ROBOROUGH

Ernest Tamblin moved to Roborough as the local wheelwright in 1910. He'd been married the previous year and their first son, Ernest, was born later that year. The family lived in the cottage on the Plymouth (right) side of the road as we see it here.

Clearly the arrival of the motor car spelt the gradual demise of horse drawn traffic and so Mr Tamblin moved with the times and opened one of the area's earliest petrol stations.

'He installed his first pump in 1930,' recalled another son, Preston, many years later.

He added that while prior to that Tamblin senior had sold petrol in two-gallon cans, 'the petrol combine as it was then known – Shell, BP, Pratts (later Esso) and National Benzole – would not supply him.

'The alternative was to go red and sell ROP (Russian Oil Products) at that time 11d and a shilling a gallon.

'About 1932/3 when the top picture was taken, Cleveland was introduced and brought by tanker from Taunton, which often arrived late at night and then returned to Taunton.'

Cleveland, incidentally, had been established in 1920 in Manchester and Preston (the name is therefore believed to have come from the Cleveland Hills and not Cleveland, Ohio). It became a public company in 1931 and in 1938 the Anglo-American Oil Company would acquire a major interest in Cleveland Petroleum Products.

Top: Claude Tamblin, son of Ernest Tamblin (who had been the local wheelwright) cycling through his father's filling station in the early thirties. Bottom: A later shot with BP, Shell and other petrols now on offer.

CAMEL'S HEAD GARAGE

Camel's Head garage, Wolseley Road.

This was erected as a tram shed, by Devonport Corporation, in 1901 to house the (tram) cars introduced to service the new Camel's Head to Saltash Passage line. However two years later the embankment was raised and it was possible to join this section to the main system. This meant that the separate depot was no longer required for its original purpose and the shed was used instead to store broken trams.

In the late 1920s the building was repurposed as Camel's Head Garage, it's address, Harbour View, Wolseley Road.

Sometime around 1937 it was taken on by 50-year-old Edwin Henry Clarke,

Other early garage proprietors in and around Wolseley Road included Arthur Burnett, who ran the Arcadia Garage for a number of years, and Sydney De Viell, who took it on in the mid-1930s. As well as John and Stephen Dyer who had Dyer's Garage.

There was also Taylor's Enterprise Garage at Milehouse and William Stower on Wolseley Road itself.

GOAD BROTHERS, PLYMPTON

Richard Venning Goad was born on the other side of the Tamar, in Anthony in 1846 he had an older sister Mary, and brother, William, and in time two younger brothers John and George. As it transpired William, like his father, would stay in Cornwall, while in 1880, a few years after John's early death, Richard would set up, with George, as Goad Brothers, Coach and Carriage Builders, in Plympton. George, sadly, would also die young, aged 34, in 1890, but the name Goad Brothers would persist for many years.

Initially they dealt in pony traps, four wheeled phaetons, landaus, dogcarts, jingles and the like (a trap being a two or four wheeled sporty cart with face to face or back to back seating; a phaeton, an open carriage; a landau a covered carriage; a dogcart being a two wheeled horse drawn cart with cross seats back to back and a jingle a kind of covered carriage). In time however the Goad enterprise embraced the combustion engine and in 1914 they were advertising themselves as sole agents for Harley Davidson. A few years later they were operating a bus service at Plympton St Mary. Using the name Ensign Coaches their buses ran between Plymouth and Cornwood. This was a time of intense competition for motor bus operators, it was a rapidly expanding market and one in which many smaller outfits were being bought out by more ambitious concerns. So it was that in May 1927 Goad's entered talks with Devon Motor Transport (established in 1919), who subsequently took them over before being swallowed up themselves later that same year by the National Omnibus and Transport Company – later to be Western National).

Goad Brothers however continued to trade for many years.

1927 May, Goad Brothers Garage, Plympton. One last hurrah before they sold the bus part of the business.

Left and below: Ridgeway Garage, Plympton. In 1925 they were advertising the new Chrysler Six: 'fitted with the latest type of all weather body work, hydraulic brakes and balloon tyres' - £455. 'Trial with pleasure.' Bottom: Garage at St Mary's Bridge.

DEVONSHIRE GARAGE, TORPOINT

AA (Arthur) Devonshire was a man with an eye to the future. Born in 1877 he started out as a cycle maker and like so many others who had started out in that industry quickly embraced the motor cycle and the motor car.

Aware of the likely impact of the latter, he bought three plots in the burgeoning Beatrice Terrace in Torpoint and, in 1913, erected a tin shed to serve as a garage adjacent to his shop. From the shop he sold all sorts including rifles, Zonophones (early records and their players) and bicycles (some of which he built himself).

The first person in Torpoint to register his business for a phone line, he was telephone No2 – the Telephone Exchange itself was No1. He and his son used to travel up to Old Trafford Park, Manchester to purchase Model T Ford commercial vehicles to bring down to Torpoint to sell.

At the end of the Great War he bought a surplus army hut, from Tregantle, which he had put up alongside his garage. It became the family home.

He later moved to Tremayne Terrace and in 1939 was stated to be the secretary of the garage that still bore his name.

Above right: William Morgan's Omega Garage at the entrance to Torpoint, the first and last in the county for those travelling on the Torpoint Ferry. Top left: AA (Arthur) Devonshire posing outside his garage in Beatrice Terrace, alongside a Calthorp motorbike, with sidecar, and his son Arthur and daughter Winifred. Parked behind him is the Borough Surveyor, Rowland Beaumont at the wheel of his Paragon motor car. Bottom left: Another view of Devonshire's Garage which, like the Omega Garage, sold Pratt's Motor Spirit.

MORE MOTOR AGENTS & GARAGES

The garages mentioned on the previous pages by no means covers all of those trading locally prior to 1939, there were also:

ARGYLE: Salem Street, run by Reginald Ellis from at least 1925.

BAKER'S: Started in Mill Street, then Ferry Road, Devonport, moved to Crownhill in 1929 when the road widening scheme was implemented. Run by Randolph Baker.

BRITANNIA: Mileshouse, run by Bawden & Pengelly.

BROADRICK: Stopford Place, run by Charles Broadrick.

FRED FOOT: Prince Rock, Embankment Road, from 1935.

FRIARY: Greenbank Terrace, proprietor RG Atkinson.

GRANT'S: Compton, Mannamead and Roborough – the oldest established firm of Motor Engineers in the District, AA & RAC appointed … Breakdown Ambulance Always Ready – within five minutes of the Airport. Run by Albert Edward Grant.

HELLINGS: Princess Street Ope, run by Alfred Hellings.

MANNAMEAD: Elm Road. Started by Simeon Robins in the early 1880s as livery stables, handed on to his son Harold.

MAYFLOWER: 70 Union Street, main Trojan dealers.

MILLBAY PARK: Robert Gully.

MUTLEY: Station Road, run by John Henry Lillicrap.

M THOMAS: Mutley Plain, works/commercials Woolster Street

NICHOLLS, JJ: Laira, James Joseph Nicholls, from early 1920s.

PLYMSTOCK: Dean Cross, from late 1920a, Paul Jacoby.

POMPHLETT: Opposite Plymstock station, from early 1920s, H Holmes, then John Francis Stephens.

RAGLAN: Run by Cload out of the Shakespeare Hotel, 1920s.

RENDLE: Elm Road, Frederick Rendle from early 1920s.

SANDERS: Manor Street, Reginald Sanders from late 1920s.

SERVICE MOTOR CO: Regent Street, Percival Clarkson.

SHAW & BURROWS: John Shaw, formerly Hyde Park Garage, Townsend Hill, c1920 moved to Frankfort Square late 1920s.

SWEET: Tavistock Place, James Sweet, from late 1930s.

TAMAR MOTOR: St Aubyn Street, Ernest Luxton from c1917.

VICTORIA: Stoke, Devonport, William Ashford from 1920.

WESTMINSTER: Gooseberry Lane. Jones/Cuming.

WINDSOR: Clemow, Mutley Road.

Other names in the trade included Annis, Bearne, Briggs, Brock, Chard, Chapman (Frank), Chapman (Richard), Damerell, De Viell, Dowling, Down, Dunn, Earl, Furzeland, Gill, Glebe, Jackman, Luckhurst, Moon, Oakden, Peachy, Petherick, Retter, Runnell & Rogers, Ryan, Skinnard, Splar, Stacey, Stephens, Taylor, Truscott, Ware, Whitfield, and Wilton.

Many of these names will feature in subsequent volumes of *Plymouth in the Age of the Petrol-Driven Motor Car.*

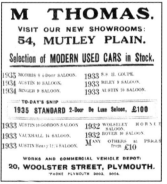

Selection of 1930s adverts: M Thomas, 1936; Mayflower, 1932; Grant's Garages, 1938, Seaton Garage, 1932 and Peter Gurney, 1927.

ROAD IMRPOVEMENTS

As the amount of road traffic carried on escalating so there was increasing pressure to improve public highways up and down the country. The creation of the Embankment at the beginning of the nineteenth century had greatly improved the eastern egress and entrance to Plymouth but road users 100 years on were more plentiful and their vehicles more substantial. Prior to the construction of the Embankment the eastern exit from Plymouth had been down Lipson Hill and through Laira. With toll houses still functioning and Laira having been absorbed by Plymouth there was an appetite to improve the route through Lipson and Laira. In February 1912 plans for carrying out this work appeared in the local press who reported on the imminent improvements to be 'effected by "unemployed" labour at the Old Laira-road for which the Local Government Board have sanctioned an application by the Plymouth Town Council to borrow £5,000, and made a grant of £250 to the funds of the Distress Committee.'

This was slightly ahead of the setting up of the Government's Road Board, which came into being in 1914.

Top and middle left: February 1912, pictures showing the proposed new route through Laira. Bottom left; April 1923, the work progresses. Above: The scene at Laira in 1938.

This new body went on to tax those motorists using the roads, with the intention of using that revenue to fix and improve existing roads and fund the creation of new ones.

Four years of international war saw the project stutter somewhat, as attention and resources were focussed elsewhere. After the war the Road Board was superseded by the Ministry of Transport and in 1922 an announcement was made about a nationwide network of what were termed 'A' and 'B' roads. The A roads numbered 1-6 were to emanate from London in a clockwise sequence, with 1 heading north, 2 heading east and 3 heading west, hence the A 38 which was to pass through Plymouth. The A roads 7-9 each stemmed from Edinburgh.

The 1920s thus saw a programme of road improvements here and elsewhere, along with a dramatic increase in the number of road users. However no-one at the time was prepared to go quite as far as the politician Lord Montagu (founder and editor of *The Car Illustrated*) who proposed inner city motorways on viaducts and a grand motorway connecting London and Liverpool, passing through Coventry, Birmingham, Wolverhampton, Stoke and Manchester.

1923 Road widening at the George Hotel, Plympton.

Top and middle: Hender's Corner 1923, 'The widening of the road at Compton proceeds apace, and these photographs indicate the character of the improvement to one of the main approaches to Plymouth.' WDM Bottom: Widening the main road at Hartley.

161

Throughout the 1920s improvements carried on apace. Aware of the impact such changes had on their readers, as old highways and byways were widened and improved, the press regularly covered the changes. Doubtless older inhabitants would have looked on in awe wondering what the future held.

Prior to the arrival of the motor car there had been little need to change the connections between communities. The passage of such road traffic as there was, meant that blockages at bottlenecks were few and far between and, such as there were, would only involve slow moving traffic and there was unlikely to be much in the way of travellers' agitation.

With no formal highway code there was a general reliance on a largely unwritten set of rules of the road, one of the prime considerations of nineteenth century travel being the width of the wheels being used on carts and coaches – anything too narrow tending to cut through those road surfaces yet to have the stoney macadam solution applied.

Top left: 1923, February, widening a narrow road in Lipson. Middle: 1925 February, further improvements to Embankment Road. Bottom: 1924, February, work completed on Hartley-hill (sic). Above: 1925 March, widening in the wake of the removal of the toll gate at Millbridge.

However, following the arrival of the motor car such rough surfaces were not necessarily tyre friendly and many were they that were grateful to the British engineer Edgar Hooley who noticed that tar spilled on the roadway surface not only kept the dust down but also led to the creation of a smooth surface.

In 1901 Hooley patented a combination of tar and Macadam's aggregate – 'Tarmac' – a recipe that would later be revised with the addition of quantities of Portland cement, pitch and resin. Of course the more motor car friendly the roads became the more motorists were able to accelerate and drive their machines at ever increasing speeds. Good news for those who could afford them and were able access parts of the country that the railway didn't reach. However it was not always such good news for the pedestrian and that way of life that took its name from that shank's pony pace – 'pedestrian.'

The question was now 'how fast is too fast?' After all it wasn't long before these new machines could easily exceed existing limits.

Above: 1927 16 August 'At many points in Devon and Cornwall schemes of road widening are being carried out, and this view shows a desirable improvement near Bickington on the Exeter-Plymouth Road.'
Right: Three stages of improvement on Manadon Hill,

SPEED KILLS

The early generation of motor cars had few of the refinements that they later acquired: electric headlamps (1908), automated windscreen wipers (1921), heater (1926), and flashing indicator lights (1935) to name but a few, and although the first speedometers started to appear just after the dawn of the twentieth century, they were by no means standard, however speed traps were, from the very beginning, a source of revenue and frustration.

So too was the speed limit itself. In 1912, 12 miles an hour was deemed to be too fast for busy inner city roads and 25 miles an hour too fast on open roads. However the means by which drivers were held to account was relatively primitive.

In July 1909, in a case typical of the time, Charlotte Gladys Carlyon was clocked covering a quarter of a mile stretch in 35 seconds, 'which was,' according to PC Osborne, 'the rate of 25 miles 1,257 yards per hour.'

Police Constable Steer, who was at the other end of the trap corroborated and said the road was quite clear at the time. 'When stopped, the defendant said she did not know what speed she was travelling at as she had no speed indicator.'

At the same County Session, Robert Dowering of Plymouth was charged with driving at 25 mph. Robert was, it transpired a very experienced driver, 'who had driven through London and many large towns in the North.' He was also a founder member of the Devon Automobile Club and his car did indeed have a speedometer, moreover one that the defendant felt was reading about 17-18 mph when he'd last checked it and he certainly hadn't speeded up.

Dowering 'was given the opportunity of measuring the piece of road, and the watches being produced, the defendant said he was quite satisfied with the way in which they worked.'

On being cross examined PC Steer said he was in the hedge concealed in the bushes; he did not have to get up to see the signal. Immediately he saw it he started his watch going ...

There followed a long debate in the court room on the quality of the police stopwatches, the potential difficulty in stopping the watch at precisely the moment the car reached a spot 25 yards from the police officer.

Furthermore Dowering claimed that stopping when waved down by the police constable had been straightforward and that he had pulled up 'within 12 yards without putting any extra pressure on the brakes,' and there had been 'no necessity to jam the brakes on and tear the car to pieces – no motorist in their right mind would do that.'

Renowned local timekeeper Frank Davis (watchmaker and Crownhill Garage proprietor) was brought in as a witness and he said that the system of timing used by the police was 'thoroughly unreliable.'

He claimed that 'as soon as a car approached the constable standing behind the bush had to do two things: he had to stand up – for if he was already standing up he would be seen by the motorists – and wave his flag with one hand and set his watch going with the other.'

Ten years earlier Davis had given evidence in a case of speeding in Beaumont Road. On that occasion he had claimed the timepieces were reliable. Back in 1902 the motor car was viewed 'by many people with bias and prejudice' claimed Percy Pearce (solicitor for and member of the Devon Automobile Club). Defending Sidney Kneebone, a driver in the employ of the Plymouth Motor Car Company, Pearce complained that his client had been unable to call passengers on his behalf. Kneebone claimed he was driving his vehicle at no more than seven or eight miles an hour, nevertheless he was fined £2 or he could serve fourteen days.

Later that year Kneebone was the driver of a bus that ran over and killed seven-year-old, Stanley Hocking. However on that occasion it was agreed that the lad had jumped out into the road from a horse bus without looking to see if it was safe to do so and that Hocking was not at fault. It was Plymouth's first motoring fatality.

Above: Is this an exercise in timing the speed of motor cars just outside Roborough?
Left: St Jude's Church and Beaumont Road before it became a very busy thoroughfare.

POLICING THE TRAFFIC

In the summer of 1923 traffic levels in Plymouth were becoming an increasing matter for concern and in order to properly assess the situation traffic was monitored across several days at three key junctions. At the Old Town Street junction with Treville Street, at Drake Circus, further up Old Town Street, and at Derry's Clock, in George Street. A principal concern was the increasing number of motor vehicles on the road and problems that posed for horses, pedestrians and the police.

It will be noted that while hand carts and horse drawn vehicles are recorded separately, there is no distinction between motor cars, vans and lorries.

It would appear that the census was overseen by the Chief Constable of Plymouth, Herbert Sanders. Sanders had been appointed, on a £600 p/a salary back in 1917 and was keen to relieve his men from point duty and traffic control as much as possible.

Side panel images this page and opposite: stills from early 1920s film showing traffic flow around George Street, Bank of England Place and Derry's Clock. Above: Looking across Union Street to the gates of the Royal Naval Hospital.

The records were presented by Sanders to the Local Taxation Committee of the House of Commons on Wednesday 4 July 1923 'in connection with the application contained in the Corporation Bill empowering the police to enforce signals regulating street traffic.'

The report in the *Western Morning News* went on to display the statistics provided in the report. These were 'prepared each day periods of two hours, beginning 9am and closing at 5pm.

'On Monday, June 18, the record taken at Treville-street shows that there was very little variation in the volume of traffic in the different periods, and the same condition observable on the other days and at the other 'points.'

On June 18 the Treville-street figures were:

9am to 11am	1,320
11am to 1pm	1,333
1pm to 3pm	1,397
3pm to 5pm	1,412
Total	5,462

'These included 314 handcarts, 36 horses, 1,698 motor cars, 244 motor cycles, 1,015 bicycles, 1,114 trams, and 1,041 horse vehicles.

Looking east along George Street, with the Theatre Royal on the right and Derry's Clock in the centre. Bank of England Place is behind the second car on the left.

The George Street junction with Bank of England Place and Union Street. Top: Policeman directing one of the first generation of Plymouth Corporation motor buses, a solid-wheeled Straker-Squire. Bottom: A new van promoting Sterling Radio Apparatus – the radio then being the very latest technology. Just above the policeman's raised hand we can see one of the first new road signs for the A389.

At Drake-circus the same day there was a total of 4,981:

9am to 11am	1,290
11am to 1pm	1,256
1pm to 3pm	1,203
3pm to 5pm	1,232

'Handcarts numbered 299, horses 6, motor cars 1,759, motor cycles 275, bicycles 896, trams 1,111, and horse vehicles 635. George-street gave total 4,898, the 'period' returns being 1,224, 1,269, 1,107, and 1,298, while the traffic comprised 342 handcarts, 7 horses, 1.714 motor cars, 183 motor cycles, 780 bicycles, 1,119 trams, and 753 horse vehicles.

'On the following day, Tuesday, one of the market-days of the week, considerable increase is shown in the figures, especially in the number of horse vehicles. At the Treville-street 'point' there was a total traffic of 7,046, of which 433 were handcarts, 45 horses, 2,078 motor cars, 461 motor cycles, 1,583 bicycles, 1,103 trams, and 1,343 horse vehicles

'At Drake-circus the total was 5,974, namely, 437 handcarts, 13 horses 1,935 motor cars, 376 motor cycles, 1,210 bicycles, 1 106 trams, and 897 horse vehicles. '

'George-street recorded 5,425, comprising 320 handcarts, 4 horses, 1,714 motor cars, 324 motor cycles, 1,083 bicycles, 1,100 trams, and 880 horse vehicles.

'On Monday and Tuesday the following week it is a noticeable fact that at each of the three census stations the traffic on the former day exceeded that on the previous Monday, while the traffic on the second day was lower than the 19th.

'At Treville-street the total on the 25th was 6,950, against 5,462; at Drake-circus 5,627 as against 4,981; and at George-street 5,798, against 5,425. On the 26th the totals were: Treville-street 6,415, compared with 7,406. Drake-circus 5,924, compared with 5,974. George-street 5,357, compared with 5,425.'

No record appears to have been taken on Wednesday, the 27th, that day being the 'early closing' day, but further statistics were prepared of the remaining three days of the week. They showed the following totals:

	Thurs	Fri	Sat
Treville-street	6,832	6,917	7,023
Drake Circus	6,287	6,536	6,380
George-street	5,709	6,305	5,571

'Although the aggregate amount of traffic varied little, it was ascertained by the census that the number of motor cars and motor cycles on the road was, generally speaking, greater on Saturdays than on other days, and as this might have a possible bearing on the question of street accidents, it would be interesting to know which days such occurrences most frequently happen. The following table shows comparison of the motor-driven conveyances and bicycles, in addition to the trams (c 1,100):

TREVILLE-STREET	Motor Cars	Motor Cycles	Bicycles
Monday, 18th	1,663	244	1,015
Tuesday, 19th	2,078	461	1,583
Monday, 25th	2,056	399	1,543
Tuesday, 26th	1,937	292	1,341
Thursday, 28th	2,030	400	1,485
Friday, 29th	2,115	435	1,511
Saturday, 30th	2,247	472	1,601
DRAKE-CIRCUS			
Monday, 18th	1,759	275	896
Tuesday, 19th	1,935	376	1,210
Monday, 25th	1,918	321	1,282
Tuesday, 26th	2,000	351	1,235
Thursday, 28th	2,061	400	1,249
Friday, 29th	2,173	423	1,367
Saturday, 30th	2,038	483	1,258
GEORGE-STREET			
Monday, 18th	1,714	183	780
Tuesday, 19th	1,714	324	1,083
Monday, 25th	1,777	336	1,193
Tuesday, 26th	1,643	315	1,042
Thursday. 28th	1,729	306	1,194
Friday, 29th	1,938	370	1,298
Saturday, 30th	1,780	355	1,296

Quite what impact all these findings had in the short term is not clear but undoubtedly Plymouth was not alone in its experiences. Chief Constable Sanders had only the previous year been granted a motor vehicle for his own use (he was allowed £100 per annum, plus licence and insurance but he was required to provide a driver at his own expense).

In 1927, his tenth year in the post, Sanders was awarded an upgrade to a new 14hp Bean saloon. The vehicle was purchased through the Princess Motor Company, although curiously enough he took delivery of the car on a visit to New Scotland Yard – Sanders had been detective inspector there before his appointment to the Plymouth job.

By this time, incidentally, there had already been a number of major changes to Plymouth's traffic management issues and yet more were in the pipeline.

Top: Chief Inspector Sanders with his 14hp Bean saloon. Bean at one point in the early 1920s outsold Austin and Morris, their Plymouth outlet was in George Street.

169

SAFETY IN THE STREETS

Two years on from the circumstances that had prompted Plymouth's 1923 traffic census the situation had become much worse. A flavour of the various concerns was expressed in a revealing article published in the *Western Morning News* in August 1925:

'As in other big centres, in Plymouth the traffic problem grows daily, and anyone who watches to-day the unending stream of traffic, particularly motor traffic, through the borough's narrow and congested streets, cannot fail to feel apprehensive.

'It generally recognized that the police are faced with a most unenviable task, and that the town's casualty list is not far more severe than it is, is due to the very capable manner which they handle the traffic under the most difficult circumstances.

'Plymouth is handicapped by narrow streets. This is the most obvious difficulty, and under the growing volume of traffic it is a problem which will have to be even more strenuously tackled in the future.

'Talk to any motorist about the Plymouth traffic and he or she will at once reply, "Well, look at your narrow, winding streets through the main part of the town." From Drake-circus to Derry's Clock, which embraces the hub of Plymouth's activities, corners and cross-streets of the utmost difficulty have to be negotiated. There is Drake-circus itself, there are the cross-streets the top of Treville-street, and the whirl of traffic round about St Andrew's Church from half a dozen directions. After the narrow channel for the first part of Bedford-street there is the sharp turn from Westwell-street, then it widens out once more for a few yards to the top of George-street where the flow of traffic from the cross-streets at the bottom Cornwall-street mingle with that using the main arteries.

'Then, of course, there are the trams in Old Town-street, and these again link with the traffic at Derry's Clock. There can be no question that the problem has been enormously increased by the heavy bus traffic, and in this direction a representative of the *Western Morning News* was yesterday given some figures by the Devon Motor Transport Company, which afford a clear and startling idea how the 'buses have added to the road traffic problem.

'Since January to the end of July the company's buses in Devon have covered about 750,000 miles, carrying about 1,200,000 passengers, Most of that traffic is to and from Plymouth.

'The Plympton trips alone involve about 4,750 miles a week, Ivybridge 3,300 miles. During the same period last year their buses carried 791,000 passengers and covered 428,000 miles, so it will be seen that the traffic from this concern alone has enormously increased. One has also to remember the 'bus traffic apart from this company, and the hundreds of charabancs in the streets of Plymouth every week. Then again, the ordinary private motor traffic is being increased every week.

'How shall the problem be tackled? Yesterday our representative sought the views of some motorists and big motor firms on the subject, but to them like most others, it seems almost insoluble.' How would a plimsoll or safety line help? There appears to be considerable doubt as to its utility, especially in such narrow streets as Plymouth possesses. Such a line around corners, they agree, might be of service, but certain parts of the main streets are so narrow that it would simply mean, if rigidly adhered to, that there would be a line of up traffic and a line of down traffic, and the fastest vehicle would have to take its pace from the slowest.

'In the opinion of the manager of one big concern, the system of issuing driving licences is altogether wrong. There should, in his opinion, be an efficiency test for drivers as well as a test for eyesight and driving; trams should be kept from the main streets, and pedestrians, like drivers, should be more educated in the regulations.

'Take your main streets any morning or afternoon when the vehicular traffic is at its height. The pedestrian traffic on the pavements is hopelessly mixed up that I guarantee, walking about three miles an hour going from Drake-circus to the Clock you will have to step off the pavement a score of times.

'Another fact which often leads to congestion, if not an actual block in the traffic, is the habit some motorists or cyclists have of leaving their car or cycle standing outside a shop in the main street for an hour or so.

'Mr. R. Humm mentioned the system adopted in Stockholm and Christiana. In the main streets there one found various safety lines. There were the lines for pedestrians, lines for cyclists, lines for slow traffic, and lines for motors. But that, of course could not be arranged in Plymouth's narrow, twisting streets.

'The experiment of the 'safety' line, say, from Bedford-street into George-street might well be tried. A broad white line running down that street for the up and down traffic would afford practical endeavour in the solution of a problem which has to be faced, and the sooner the better.'

The following year a similar experiment that had been put in place in Birmingham a few years earlier, was officially recognised and middle of the road white line markings, first mooted in Michigan, on the other side of the Atlantic back in 1911, were gradually introduced here in the 1930s, with the first broken line down the centre of a road being laid down on a 70 mile stretch of the A30 and A38 in Devon in 1935.

White lines were also introduced as 'stop' lines at junctions.

'In view of the large amount of traffic passing daily along Bedford-street and George-street, where is one of the most congested corners in the West of England, the adoption of a "Plimsoll" line enabling drivers of motors and other vehicles to keep to the correct part of the road would reduce risk of accident to a minimum.'

From the WMN *30 November 1926: TRAFFIC SAFEGUARD - An illuminated sign for directing Plymouth traffic by night, the idea of the Chief Constable of Plymouth (Mr WH Sanders). Plymouth is probably the first town in Great Britain to install these aids to night traffic.*

PLYMOUTH'S FIRST ONE WAY STREET

14 October 1926 north-bound traffic is directed around the western side of Drake Circus.

1 February 1927. 'Sorry sir you can't come this way anymore, George Street is now a one-way street ... and it's not this way!' The original newspaper caption noted that 'the policemen on duty at either end of the thoroughfare were busily engaged in directing drivers of vehicles to the proper routes.'

The first permanently enforced one-way street of the modern traffic era was designated in Mare Street, Hackney by the Metropolitan Commissioner of Police, in August 1924. Under the terms of the restrictions, traffic was only allowed to proceed in a southerly direction between Amhurst Road and Dalston Lane. Two years later, on Thursday 14 October 1926 Plymouth's first experiment in one-way traffic commenced.

'According to the plan the island of shops which, at the bottom of the hill, divides Tavistock-road from Old Town-street, will split the traffic. All traffic moving upwards in the direction of North-hill and Mutley will pass up though Old Town-street, and all the traffic coming down the hill will enter Drake-circus via Tavistock-road.

'Another one-way street will be Saltash-street, which will only be used by upward traffic, and this traffic coming along Cobourg-street and wishing to get into Old Town-street will have to make its entry down Tavistock-road.'

As it transpired George Street was not far behind, as just over three months later, from 1 February 1927 it too became a designated one way thoroughfare. Others followed suit, and indeed 'one way traffic was inaugurated in Marlborough-street, Devonport' before 1926 had drawn to a close. The new situation there meant that 'all northern-bound traffic was diverted through King-srteet, and all southern-bound traffic by way of Marlborough-street, which narrow thoroughfare was very considerably relieved.'

The original Drake Circus experiment incidentally was described as being 'one of the most important which the committee has undertaken, but, as Alderman Modley pointed out to our (*Western Morning News*) representative, the growth of vehicular traffic in Plymouth has been so tremendous and the streets are so narrow that drastic action is necessary.'

Alderman William Modley was chairman of the Watch Committee which in turn was the parent body of the Traffic Committee and it was remarkable that in just one generation petrol-driven vehicles had had such a massive impact on the city's streets.

Old Town Street and George Street were by no means isolated examples: 'In Plymouth one of the worst streets for congestion of traffic is Exeter-street leading up into Treville-street, and entering the stream of traffic coming down Old Town Street. For the most part this traffic is horse-drawn. It is felt that it would be an admirable thing if all that traffic from the east end of the town could be diverted in Exeter-street, so as to cross the North Quay and pass up Notte-street.'

The report in the local press continued: 'The growth of Plymouth's traffic must be apparent to even the most casual observer, but perhaps some better realisation of its size will be gathered when it is stated that at the present time something like 700 buses arrive and leave Plymouth in the course of every week-day. One has but to add to that the charabanc traffic, the ordinary business traffic, and the enormous growth of private car traffic to get some idea of the problem.

'In dealing with the safety of pedestrians the opinion held is that many people are involved in street accidents through their own carelessness. But this is more a matter for education than for legislation.

'It may not be generally known what is being done in Plymouth towards educating the public on safety in the streets. Very shortly a further series of lectures on the subject will be given by a member of the police force to scholars in the day schools and by the end of the winter approximately 20,000 children will have received instruction. In addition, the 'Safety First' film will shortly be on view at kinema houses.'

Two pictures taken seconds apart but ten years after George Street was first designated one way and still policemen are needed to direct the traffic here and elsewhere.

PLYMOUTH'S FIRST TRAFFIC LIGHTS

As we now march through the third decade of the 21st century considering the prospect not only of electric cars but also of driverless vehicles, spare a thought, if you will, for the situation motorists faced a century ago, towards the end of the third decade of the 20th century.

There were, of course, far fewer vehicles on our roads, but there were already far more than existing arrangements at that time were able to cope with. More often than not those arrangements involved an often exasperated and weary-armed policeman on point duty, standing in the middle of the road stopping traffic, and then waving it on this way and that.

1935: A white gloved policeman on point duty directs traffic at the junction of Russell Street, Cornwall Street, Bedford Street and Frankfort Street.

In Cleveland, Ohio there had been an experiment with red and green lights, used in conjunction with a warning buzzer, back in 1914. Almost a decade later the French adopted a sound and light combination in Paris on the junction of the Grand Boulevard and the Boulevard de Strasbourg. This involved a hand operated light hanging from a lamp-post with the word HALTE inscribed on a glass lens, with someone beating a gong each time the light was about to be switched on or off.

London followed suit soon afterwards, with their first electronically illuminated traffic sign going up at the junction of St James's Street and Piccadilly in July 1926. They opted to follow the red, amber and green light system that had been introduced in New York in 1918.

However those London lights were still being operated manually and it wasn't until Guy Fawkes Day, 5 November 1927, that the country's first set of automatic traffic lights was installed – at the Princess Square crossroads in Wolverhampton.

Thereafter they soon sprang up around the busier junctions across Britain's cities and in the summer of 1929, on Tuesday 6 August, Plymouth was blessed with its first set. Although it's hard now to imagine life without them and yes, we can all think of some we could do without, it's interesting to reflect now on how this momentous occasion was reported in the local press at the time: 'Plymouth's first experience yesterday of automatic traffic control signals in Old Town-street, where Treville-street and East-street join the main road, was certainly a success.

'This is admittedly one of the worst junctions in the city, and the policemen on point duty there invariably have had an arduous task.

'Old Town-street is not particularly wide, considering that it carries two sets of tramlines and is part of the main road through the city, and Treville-street and East-street are frankly narrow, and are difficult streets to negotiate.

Plymouth's first automatic traffic lights, where Old Town Street meets East Street.

'This means, in effect, that he must give way to the cross traffic, and in no circumstances proceed straight ahead.
'If the red and amber lights area shining together, he should presume that in a very few seconds they will give way to green, and he will be able to proceed straight ahead while the cross traffic is held up. Vice-versa, if the green and amber lights are shining together, the driver should know that in a few seconds they will give way to red, which means "Stop."
'For some time yesterday Supt. Coombes (Deputy Chief Constable), Supt. Denley, Mr WHJ Priest (chairman of the Watch Committee) and other experts on traffic watched the proceedings at the top of Treville-street and made experiments with the duration of signals, and in due course, no doubt, a workable scheme will be evolved.'

'In future the human control is to be replaced by an automaton, and drivers of vehicles will have to rely largely on their common sense and a common understanding rather than on the sympathy of a policeman.
'Yesterday a squad of special policemen helped the motorists and drivers of horse vehicles to understand that a "stop" signal directly ahead of them does not of necessity mean that they must stop. They explained also that an all-clear signal does not always mean that traffic from the side turnings has been stopped.
'The system has proved successful at Exeter. At strategic points in each of the four crossroads is an indicator on which are three lamps. They are coloured red, amber, and green, and they mean respectively "Stop," "Caution," and "Go." A driver approaching the cross-roads sees on his left hand one of these indicators. If it is at "Stop" he knows – or should do – that the signal for the cross traffic is "Go."

1937 Coronation time in Fore Street, Devonport, note the traffic lights, on the left, on the corner of Tavistock Street, with JC Tozers store this side and the Prince George on the other.

SAFETY FIRST

As roads became busier so the necessity for a set of rules and regulations that could be imposed on road users increased.

It wasn't until after the Great War that the Ministry of Transport was set up and the following year the Departmental Committee on the Regulation of Motor Vehicles announced that 'a compulsory and uniform code of signals for all road vehicles' was to be 'brought into operation.'

In Britain's busiest city, London, a system had already evolved whereby drivers indicated to fellow road users that were about to stop, or turn right by extending their arm out of the driver's window and adopting a common signal.

This had proved so useful it was felt that it should be adopted elsewhere. Where the driver was in an enclosed cab, or on the left hand side of the vehicle because he was driving a left hand drive (typically American) car, then the use of a dummy arm was acceptable. This was also handy when it was raining.

In 1923 a booklet was published by His Majesty's Stationery Office: *Traffic Signals to be used by the Police and Drivers of Vehicles*. The booklet was produced after discourse between the Automobile Association and the Police and followed on from the creation of the London 'Safety First' Council in 1916. This in turn was a response to the 'alarming increase in road accidents' that was witnessed during the blackouts in the 1914-18 war.

A National 'Safety First' Association was established in 1926 and ten years later this became the Royal Society for the Prevention of Accidents.

'A 'block' in the traffic at the junction of Treville-street and Old Town-street, showing the difficulties which the police encounter in Plymouth's narrow thoroughfares.' Note the Bovril sign on Drake Circus. Opposite page: Pedestrians are encouraged to use recognised crossing places but it would appear motorists don't always take heed.

It was an interesting turn of events for the AA to be now giving road safety their careful consideration as the original rationale for the organisation had been to prevent their members from being caught speeding. The Association's roots are to be found in a meeting at the Lyons' Trocadero Restaurant in Shaftesbury Avenue, London, in June 1905.

Charles Jarrott had called together a collection of enthusiastic motorists with the intention of coming up with a strategy to employ scouts on cycles to patrol roads and alert members to any speed traps ahead. Initially styling themselves the Motorists' Mutual Association the following week, on 29 June members voted to change the name to the Automobile Association.

By the end of 1905 membership had reached 100, however such was the speed at which the motor car was adopted that by 1914 that number had increased to 83,000.

By this time official duties went well beyond the original remit and in addition to 'indicating dangers on the road' included 'helping motorists who had broken down.'

Agents and recommended repairers were appointed and by 1908 they were able to list some 1,500 agents in their first AA Members' Special Handbook.

Uniforms were first issued to their 'scouts' in 1909 and by 1912 the organisation had 950 cyclist patrols and introduced 'sentry' style boxes which were soon equipped with telephones allowing members to contact the AA and for the AA to contact their patrolmen.

Scouts wore a yellow armband with the letters AA on their left arm and, briefly, carried a red and white reversible circular, metal disc on the front of their coat. Showing the white side indicated that the scout was there if needed; the red side meant the driver being thus signalled was being encouraged to drive more carefully, and displayed above the head meant 'Stop Please'.

Early AA facilities, a first generation scout hut and a patrolman with his liveried motorcycle and sidecar.

'SURE SHIELD'

Although by no means the only motoring organisation of the time (the RAC dates its foundation back to 1896), the AA championed the interests of the motorist in many pioneering ways.

In addition to the on road services they provided for drivers they produced maps, guides and hotel recommendations.

With more people than ever travelling across the country by road rather than rail, there was clearly an appetite from the motorist to have an indication of where best they might find food or overnight accommodation. So it was that in 1908 the AA pledged to provide their members with information in the following year's handbook of around 1,000 of the leading hotels around the country. Furthermore they undertook to draw attention to these particular properties with a newly designed sign. The list duly appeared in the 1909 *AA Handbook*, however

Top left: The AA - the motorist's 'Sure Shield'. 1920 ad from their Exeter HQ informing all that the AA Badge protects against certain regretable incidents, including 'unecessary delay due to breakdown, lack of motor fuel, spares etc; foreign customs dues and unsatisfactory hotel accommodation.' Above: AA box 61 miles from London and 184 from Exeter.

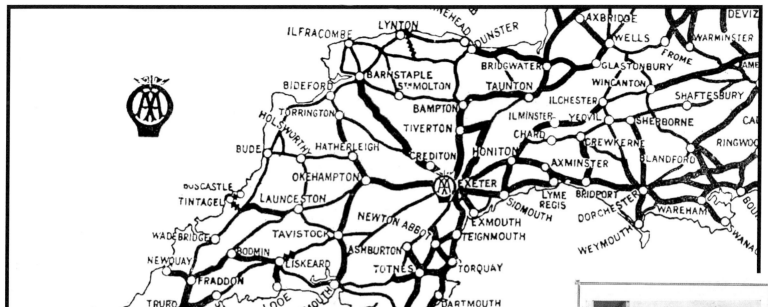

it wasn't long before the organisation decided that a rather more critical approach would help members and in 1912 the AA Secretary, Stenson Cook, adopted the star system already deployed by brandy producers – five stars were the pinnacle, three were taken as 'standard.' Needless to say inclusion in the handbook became the aim of almost every hotelier. The coveted AA sign and recommendation was a great marketing device and, unsurprisingly, inspectors were given strict instructions to accept no favours ... and to pay for themselves!

Top: '1928 MOTORING AT EASTER: Map prepared by the Automobile Association showing the condition of the road in the West. The thick lines represent good roads and the thin those which are fair. The others are either poor or bad.' Above and right: Keen to attract the motorist, the Albion Hotel and the Hoe Mansion Hotel boasting that it is AA & RAC recommended.

Hoe Mansion Hotel

A.A.   R.A.C.

AT THE GATES OF THE HOE

ELECTRIC LIFT TO ALL FLOORS

CENTRAL HEATING   BALL ROOM

RUNNING HOT & COLD WATER IN ALL BEDROOMS

GAS FIRES IN BEDROOMS

GARAGE   Telephone 533

Telegrams: " Hoe Mansions, Plymouth "

77

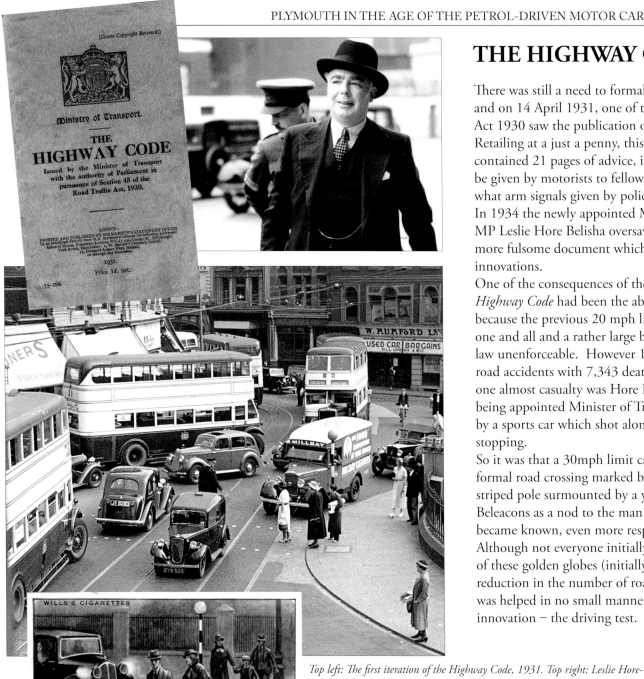

THE HIGHWAY CODE

There was still a need to formalise the rules of the road even more and on 14 April 1931, one of the provisions of the Road Traffic Act 1930 saw the publication of *The Highway Code*.

Retailing at a just a penny, this relatively slim volume nevertheless contained 21 pages of advice, including what arm signals should be given by motorists to fellow motorists and pedestrians and what arm signals given by policeman to motorists meant.

In 1934 the newly appointed Minister of Transport, Devonport MP Leslie Hore Belisha oversaw the production of a somewhat more fulsome document which brought in a couple of major innovations.

One of the consequences of the earlier incarnation of *The Highway Code* had been the abolition of the speed limit, mainly because the previous 20 mph limit in towns had been flouted by one and all and a rather large backlog of cases had rendered the law unenforceable. However 1934 witnessed a record number of road accidents with 7,343 deaths and 231,603 injuries, indeed one almost casualty was Hore Belisha himself who, shortly after being appointed Minister of Transport was narrowly missed by a sports car which shot along Camden High Street without stopping.

So it was that a 30mph limit came into being along with a new formal road crossing marked by the presence of a black and white striped pole surmounted by a yellow globe. Initially dubbed Beleacons as a nod to the man who introduced them they quickly became known, even more respectfully, as Belisha beacons.

Although not everyone initially got the concept, the introduction of these golden globes (initially they didn't flash) saw a dramatic reduction in the number of road traffic accidents. This reduction was helped in no small manner by the other great Hore Belisha innovation – the driving test.

Top left: The first iteration of the Highway Code, 1931. Top right: Leslie Hore-Belisha. Above and opposite page: 1937 a Belisha Beacon at the Old Town Street, Bedford Street junction – note the ambivalent attitude of motorists and pedestrians. Inset: Cards from the Wills Cigarette Card 'Safety First' album which had an introduction by Hore-Belisha.

Right: The Morris Ten two seate nearest the camera is a 193. registered vehicle with Wilco Robot Signalling - a driver side screen pillar with a tiny set of traffic lights indicating green when it was safe to overtake. They were made illegal the following year

BEWARE OF TRAM LINES

LOOK BEFORE YOU LEAVE
THE PAVEMENT

THE DRIVING TEST IS INTRODUCED

New Driving Test – Motorists who have a thorough knowledge of the highway code and have complete control of their cars should have little difficulty in passing the new driving test. But they should be able to reverse a car against a kerb (left), give the appropriate road signs (centre), and should be able to show the examiner that they possess sufficient road sense not to park a car in such a dangerous position as that illustrated on the right. The car is a 1929 Austin 7 with post-production bumpers and fog light.

Since it was first introduced on 1 June 1935 by the Minister of Transport (Leslie Hore-Belisha then the MP for Devonport), around 50 million driving tests have been taken in the UK. Back then, strangely enough, the roads were markedly less safe than they are today: there were over 7,300 people killed on the road 80 years ago when there were only 2.4 million vehicles on the road. Now there are more than ten times that number of vehicles but a only about a third as many deaths.

Originally there were no test centres, one just arranged to meet an examiner at an obvious location like a post office, railway station or town hall. Furthermore although the test became compulsory in June 1935, drivers were able to take a test voluntarily from 16 March that year, the idea being to try and avoid a mad rush on the first day of June. Keen to keep their readers abreast of the development on 25 March 1935 a 'female reporter' from the *Western Morning News* submitted herself to the rigours of that test. This is her account: 'Yesterday I became the proud possessor of a pink certificate, and immediately developed a superiority complex towards those motorists who have not been judged competent to drive by a 'pukka' examiner authorised by the Minister of Transport to conduct tests.

'I was examined at Plymouth by Mr A Breen Searle, and although I had been driving for several months found it by no means a walk or rather drive, over. The novice will find the test a severe one, and qualifying for it will become a serious business not to be taken in hand lightly or wantonly, but those who have a complete mastery over their cars and a thorough knowledge of the highway code have little to fear. These two things are essentials, and there is no dodging either of them,

'When I had done everything required of me and answered every question put to me to the best of my ability, and was rewarded with the precious pink slip which the examiner handed to me there and then with the words, "Miss -------- I hand you this with much pleasure," I experienced a feeling of relief, and felt that I had well and truly earned the certificate and that it was of definite value as a tribute to my driving ability.

'I did not, however, feel that the certificate was indicative that I was a first-class driver, for I was conscious of short-comings, particularly in gear-changing. Slick gear-changing, however, does not appear to be the main concern of the examiner. What he is anxious to find out is whether the driver undergoing the test is safe at large on the road with a death-dealing machine.

'He wants to know if the driver is aware of his or her correct position on the road, is cognizant of the rules of the road, considerate to other road users, careful and quick to react in an emergency.

'Mr Searle requested me to stop and restart on a hill, turn round at the bottom of a steep hill I had just descended and remount the hill, reverse into an opening both to the left of it and the right, drive through traffic, and stop suddenly as if a child had dashed out into the road without warning.

'In addition, I was plied with a host of questions on the highway code and as to what I should do or should not do in certain circumstances.

'Placing his hand over the speedometer indicator Mr Searle said, "What speed are we travelling?" and I felt considerably gratified when my estimate was within a couple of miles of the exact speed. Other questions with which Mr Searle bombarded me were "How would you take a left-hand corner? How would you take a right-hand corner? What would you do if you saw an old lady crossing the road slowly and you had plenty of time to slow up? Where do you expect to see pedestrians? When would you use your horn? Is there any reason why you should not blow the horn when your car is stationary? Can you blow it when the car is at a standstill, if so, when? Is there any limit to the time when you may use your horn when the car is travelling? If you want to turn round in a road, what do you do?

'Mr Searle nearly caught me out with the question, "When you make a signal do you do anything before acting on it?

'Just in time I remembered that one naturally glances in the

'L;' for Learner plates were also introduced in June 1935 for vehicles being driven by those who had yet to pass their test. This picture of a 1935 Morris 8 with L plate, was taken in St Andrew Street.

mirror to see that the signal has been observed and nothing unexpected is happening behind.

'Another question which nearly stalled me was, "When you are overtaking what do you expect the other driver to do?"

"Pull in," I said. "Anything else? asked my tormentor. "Slow down," I added as an after-thought. "Anything else?" queried Mr Searle again. "Wave me on," with an inward sigh of relief that I had given the answer he was waiting for. Mr Searle then asked me if I should proceed after being given this signal, to which, of course, the answer is make sure the road is clear first.

'To those who have not yet passed through the mill, my advice is, "Do not attempt the spectacular or show off, the examiner will not be impressed."

'By the way, it is interesting to note that the certificate has to be signed by the driver who has passed the test in the presence of the examiner, obviously to prevent the certificate being passed on to another.'

PLYMOUTH'S FIRST CAR PARK?

The concept of a car park (or parking lot as they call them on the other side of the Atlantic) is almost as old as the motor car itself, with the first being recorded in 1898 and the first multi-storey affair in 1901, in London, just off Piccadilly Circus.

It's not at all clear where the first such facility was in Plymouth, but as car ownership mushroomed in the 1920s so the issue of where vehicles could be safely left without causing problems for moving traffic became increasingly apparent.

The chief constable was given the responsibility for advising on and supervising parking areas and it wasn't until 1934, the year so many new regulations affecting the rules of the road came into play, that the police were relieved of this burden.

One plausible contender for the city's first proper public car park is the nineteenth century Princess Square. Laid out principally by the architect John Foulston, who came to Plymouth having won a competition to design the Theatre Royal, the square was named after a visit by Princess (later Queen) Victoria.

The centrepiece, overlooked by all the buildings in the square, was a small but attractive green space lined with trees. The buildings themselves were mainly occupied as office space by a number of prosperous, professional businesses: estate agents, auctioneers, accountants, insurance brokers and solicitors.

Most working people could not then afford cars but many of these professionals could, hence no doubt not only the conversion of the central garden area to a car park, but also the decision by R Humm & Co to move their showroom site from Old Town Street to a site Plymouth Corporation were keen to redevelop – and reduce in size – on the corner of Westwell Street and Princess Square. Humms were agents for some of the more upmarket makes of motor car at that time.

Top left: Princess Square in the 1890s. Middle: Princess Square c.1911
Bottom: The parade ground at the Royal Naval Barracks, Devonport is turned into a huge car park for Navy Days in August 1929.

Princess Square 1937, some of the trees remain, but the grass is gone and a hard surface has been put in place to provide a suitable space for car parking.

Construction of the new corner showroom and office block begins. Note the car park and what was a constant stream of buses.

ROBERT HUMM

Between the wars the Humm's business flourished and Robert was able to move into an all-new showroom in Princess Square, overlooking what was possibly Plymouth's first proper car park. Princess Square at that time was surrounded by the offices of Plymouth leading solicitors, architects and accountants – the sort of professionals who could afford cars.

The site itself, on the corner of Westwell Street and Princess Square was formerly occupied by Plymouth Repertory Theatre, a Foulston building that had been erected as the Mechanic's Institute the best part of 100 years earlier.

The new showroom, with offices above, occupied a somewhat different footprint however as the Corporation had purchased the land in the arrangement to allow for a significant element of street widening – the new structure was 11ft further back from the original street line in Westwell Street and 18ft back in Princess Square. The new layout made what had been a very tight corner, on the main bus and tram route, a good deal easier.

Robert Humm himself appears to have been well liked and well connected; in his younger days he was something of a boxing enthusiast and he was a member of the Sir Francis Drake Bowling Club.

His life however came to an abrupt end in the summer of 1938. It was Thursday, 4 August, and around 5pm he left the showrooms in Princess Square and walked across Guildhall Square to catch a bus home to Houndiscombe Villas and then suddenly collapsed. A St John's Ambulance whisked him off to what was then known as the Prince of Wales's Hospital at Greenbank, but the 69-year-old Humm was pronounced dead on arrival.

The business carried on at Princess Square for a number of years, before the whole operation was concentrated on the Alexandra Road premises. The showroom here would be bought 10 years after the Blitz by Frank Vosper and Vosper's Motor House.

Above: 1937 and building work continues apace. Right:
View of the new showroom from the Guildhall Tower.

SAFETY FIRST SIGNS

CROSS ROADS
WARNING SIGN-MAIN ROAD

SIGNALS AHEAD
ON APPROACHING AUTOMATIC SIGNAL AREAS LOCK OUT FOR THIS WARNING

SLOW MAJOR ROAD AHEAD
WARNING SIGN-SUBSIDIARY ROAD

TO HALT FROM FRONT

TO HALT FROM BEHIND

TO HALT FROM FRONT AND BEHIND

TO BRING ON A HALTED VEHICLE

TO BRING ON Commencement of Signal

TO BRING ON Completion of Signal

STEEP HILL

SCHOOL

30 RESTRICTED AREA

LEVEL CROSSING Guarded

CROSSING NO GATES Unguarded

PARKING PLACE

DOUBLE BEND

DERESTRICTION SIGN

ROAD JUNCTION

ROUND ABOUT

A selection of British road signs, most fairly obvious in their imagery, although the school's 'flaming torch of knowledge' might test some.

SIGNS OF GROWTH

The British road network, like most around the world, was woefully signposted prior to the rapid increase in cycling towards the end of the nineteenth century. From the early 1880s onwards the Cyclists' Touring Club and the National Cyclists Union, both founded in 1878, started erecting their own cast-iron 'danger boards' around popular cycling routes.

Generally these signs were to warn of potential hazards, rather than to advise of distances or directions.

The cycling organisations quickly became a powerfully lobbying group and in 1888 successfully persuaded the government that responsibility for roads should be vested with county councils and funded through taxation rather than road tolls.

With the first motor cars taking to the roads here less than a decade later it was inevitable that the need to sort signage would become all the more pressing. The AA and other motoring organisations led the way, erecting their own idiosyncratic signs and warning boards across the country.

Frankfort Street c1939, note the white dots down the middle of the road, among the city's first street markings.

The Motor Car Act of 1903 saw the introduction of four national signs. Designed to sit at least eight feet above the road and 50 yards from what they were referencing, they were: a white ring indicating a speed limit (which was marked on a plate below it); a white (or occasionally red) diamond denoting a 'motor notice' – typically a weight restriction appended beneath it; a red disc, prohibiting access and a red, open triangle indicating a hazard warning.

The signs provided the basic template for the later, major revision contained in the 1934 *Road Traffic Acts and Regulations* handbook that sat alongside Hore Belisha's 1934 edition of *The Highway Code*.

Interestingly enough it also saw the government eventually embrace the use of symbols over words, a practice that had been relatively standard on the Continent since 1909.

The new regulations also spelt the end of the AA's black and yellow vitreous enamel signs, and those of the Royal Automobile Club (RAC), although they still produced temporary signage for events and the like.

Dean Cross junction, Plymstock, note on the far left one of the area's first generation of metalled direction signs, here pointing left towards Plymouth. Note also the white line down the middle of the road and the garage behind the road sign.
Six-year-old Desmond Barnes was killed here in 1937 when his trolley hit a lorry.

Spooner's Corner, c1939 , looking down Bedford Street . Above the women we see what was possibly Plymouth's first new road sign indicating that this was part of the A38.

ACKNOWLEDGEMENTS

As with any book there are always a lot of people to thank – for providing ideas, inspiration and images. Sadly I can't remember the name of the gentleman who came into our shop on the Barbican several years ago and suggested that I do a book on the garages and showrooms of Plymouth but I really hope he manages to find a copy.

For the actual compilation of material I'm enormously indebted to Anne Corry and Terry Willson. Anne, and her husband Michael, have been brilliant in sniffing out pictures and stories and back stories of early motoring and cycling pioneers, while Terry has spent hours trawling through newspaper back pages unearthing fascinating illustrated articles concerning the early impact of the motor car.

I'm also extremely grateful to Roger Armstrong, who I've never met, but through a random encounter on the A303 with a friend of his, Andrew Harding, who was towing an Austin 7, I've made his acquaintance and he has been marvellous in identifying a great many of the cars featured in this book.

Robert Crawley of the West Country Historic Omnibus Trust allowed me to share a number of brilliant images, especially those concerning the long running Mumford organisation.

During the course of working my way through this book I've also been fortunate in being able to relate some of the excellent glass plate negatives that Ron Andrew shared with me many years ago to actual events that took place in the mid-1920s.

Sandra Clemo (nee Haskell) supplied some stunning early images of Andrew's Garage, which her father took on after the war.

As ever Derek Tait has been generous in allowing access to his wonderful collection of local images.

Linda Mills shared some family photo albums, as did Alice Astor, although like Colin Rowe who did the same, in many instances there was sadly little or no information recorded as to the who, the why and the where of the photographs.

Dave Sharp's account of the Plymouth Motor Club, 1908-2008, has been extremely helpful and Keith Loze, as ever, has been brilliant in helping trawl through the *Herald* and *Western Morning News* cuttings archive and in establishing contacts within the world of motoring enthusiasts.

Thanks to the South West Image Bank, the Box and the Plymouth Barbican Trust.

Over the last 25 years I've been writing Looking Back for the *Plymouth Herald* many people have been kind enough to share pictures and stories and in no particular order I'd like also to thank: Tina Southgate, Ken Hawke, Caroline Taylor, Fernley Parker, Fernley Wallis, Liz Reardon, Dennis and Diane Collinson, Colyn Thomas, John Boulden, and Neill Mitchell.

Apologies to anyone I've missed or forgotten, rest assured no-one has been deliberately overlooked!

Thanks are also due to Gloria Dixon, Patricia Greathead and Clare Robinson for their tireless contributions in the proof reading department. Clare is also the publisher of this and all of our Pen & Ink productions and, like me, was initially sceptical about the viability of this particular project. Hopefully our fears will be unfounded, because, we now anticipate not one but three books on Plymouth in the Age of the Petrol Driven Motor Car, as there was far too much material to squeeze into just one volume.

Last but by no means least, thanks to Benji Robinson for his work on the cover design and his colourisation of the main image.

Chris Robinson MBE
November 2021

BIBLIOGRAPHY

Car – **Richard Sutton**, Dorling Kindersley *(1996)*

Devon Roads – **Michael Hawkins**, Devon Books *(1988)*

Devon Roads, Past and Present – **Valerie R Belsey**, Past and Present *(1993)*

Devon in the 1930s: The Way We Were – **Gerald Wasley**, Halsgrove (1998)

Plymouth Yesterday Today – **Vic Saundercock** (1989)

Doidge's Western Counties Illustrated Annual – (1888 -1940 inclusive)

From Rattles to Radio, A History of Plymouth City Police Force – **Ernest Dickaty**, typescript (1977)

"Get Your Skates On" Plymouth's Roller Skating Rinks – **Diana Lawer**, Three Towns (2007)

Images of Plymouth – **Tom Bowden**, Sutton Publishing (2006)

Images of England: Plymouth – **Derek Tait**, Tempus Publishing Ltd (2003)

Kelly's Devonshire Directory – (1919, 1926, 1939)

Motorcade A Dictionary of Motoring History – **Maurice A Hammond**, G Bell & Sons (1969)

100 Years of the Co-operative in Plymouth – **Chris Robinson,** Pen & Ink (2009)

Plymouth Street Directories and Guides – Various (1900-1940)

Plymouth: A New History – **Crispin Gill**, Devon Books (1993)

Plymouth: A Pictorial History – **Guy Fleming**, Phillimore & Co Ltd (1995)

Plymouth Bygones: Sixty Years of Memories and Pictures – **Guy Fleming,** Devon Books (1991)

Plymouth in the Twenties and Thirties - **Chris Robinson**, Pen & Ink (2008)

Plymouth in War & Peace – **Guy Fleming**, Bossiney Books (1987)

Plymouth: More Pictures from the Past – **Guy Fleming**, The Devonshire Press Ltd (1996)

Plymouth 100 Years of Street Travel – **RC Sambourne**, Glasney Press (circa 1970)

Premises and Facilities of the Western National and Southern National – **Robert Crawley** ed WHOTT (2017)

Plympton's Past in Pictures – **John Boulden** MBE (2007)

Safety First – Issued by WD & HO Wills (c1937)

Saltash Remembered Pt 2 – **Douglas C Vosper**, PDS (1981)

The Complete Encyclopedia of Motorcars – edited **GN Georgano**, Ebury Press (1968)

The New Shell Book of Firsts – **Patrick Robertson**, Headline (1995)

The Post Office Directory of Plymouth, Devonport, Stonehouse & District 1908, 1910-11 – Swiss & Co

The Trams of Plymouth: A 73-Year Story – **Martin Langley and Edwina Small**, Ex Libris Press (1990)

Torpoint – **Pat and Freda Manning**, Chalford (1997)

Western Morning News – (1895-1940)

Victorian Plymouth: As Time Draws On – **Chris Robinson**, Pen & Ink (1991)

Wind in the Willows – Kenneth Graham, Metheun (1931)

And then there's Wikipedia, Ancestry, the British Newspaper Archive, the AA, Grace's Guide and related websites across the internet generally!

SOME OTHER CHRIS ROBINSON TITLES AVAILABLE

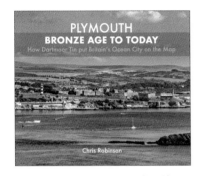

PLYMOUTH BRONZE AGE TO TODAY *How Dartmoor Tin put Britain's Ocean City on the Map*

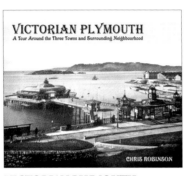

VICTORIAN PLYMOUTH *Photographic tour of the Three Towns*

PLYMOUTH'S GREAT WAR *Three Towns United in Conflict*

PLYMOUTH IN THE TWENTIES & THIRTIES

PLYMOUTH IN THE FORTIES & FIFTIES *1945-1957*

PLYMOUTH IN THE FIFTIES & SIXTIES *1957-1969*

PLYMOUTH IN THE SEVENTIES

A HISTORY OF DEVONPORT

NB: *Each title runs to 256 pages and includes around 500+ illustrations*

visit www.chrisrobinson.co.uk for further details

FORTHCOMING TITLES INCLUDE:
PLYMOUTH & THE AGE OF THE PETROL-DRIVEN MOTOR CAR 1939-1979
PLYMOUTH & THE AGE OF THE PETROL-DRIVEN MOTOR CAR 1980-Today

150 YEARS OF THE CO-OPERATIVE IN PLYMOUTH *1860-2010*